In My Lifetime

Rev. Dr. Herbert Daughtry

In My Lifetime

Towards the Presidency *of* Barack Obama

Africa World Press, Inc.

P.O. Box 1892  P.O. Box 48
Trenton, NJ 08607   Asmara, ERITREA

Africa World Press, Inc.

P.O. Box 1892　　　　　　　P.O. Box 48
Trenton, NJ 08607　　　　　Asmara, ERITREA

Copyright © 2010 Herbert Daughtry
First Printing 2010

Cover Photo: Caleb Miller
Book design: Guenet Abraham

All rights reserved. No part of this publication may be reproduced, stored in a retrieval system or transmitted in any form or by any means electronic, mechanical, photocopying, recording or otherwise without the prior written permission of the publisher.

Library of Congress Cataloging-in-Publication Data

Daughtry, Herbert.
　In my life time : towards the presidency of Barack Obama / Herbert Daughtry.
　　　p. cm.
　Compilation of articles previously published in the Daily challenge.
　Includes bibliographical references and index.
　　ISBN 1-59221-741-9 (hard cover) -- ISBN 1-59221-742-7 (pbk.)　1. Presidents--United States--Election--2008. 2. Political campaigns--United States--History--21st century. 3. United States--Politics and government--2001-2009. 4. Obama, Barack. I. Title.
　E906.D38 2010
　973.932092--dc22
　　　　　　　　　　　　　　　　　　　2009048447

Dedication

I dedicate this book to the Daughtry family ...
my wife, Karen; my children, from last to first:
Herbert Jr., Dawn, Sharon, and Leah;
my son- and daughter-in-law: Todd and Danielle;
and my grandchildren: Myles, Herbert III, and Lorenzo.

I love you all ... let us continue to honor the covenant.

CONTENTS

xi Acknowledgments
xiii Introduction

Chapter One

3 *Super Tuesday to the End of the Democratic Primaries, February 2008-June 2008*

SUPER TUESDAY OBAMA OR CLINTON: WHICH WAY BLACK AMERICA?
ALAS POOR HILLARY, THE MYSTERIES ARE AGAINST THEE!
SHOWDOWN AT THE RULES AND BYLAWS COMMITTEE MEETING
THE ELECTION HEARD AROUND THE WORLD

Chapter Two

31 *Inside the 2008 Democratic National Convention— Putting it All Together*

FRIDAY, AUGUST 22—*Convention Thoughts, Arrival in Denver, Podium Preview Party*

SATURDAY, AUGUST 23—*Joe Biden Named as Obama's Vice President, Credentials & Skyboxes*
SUNDAY, AUGUST 24—*The Interfaith Gathering*
MONDAY, AUGUST 25—*African American Caucus Meeting, Convention Opening Session*
TUESDAY, AUGUST 26—*Hillary Clinton's Speech*
WEDNESDAY, AUGUST 27—*Bill Clinton's and Joe Biden's Speeches, and the Roll Call Vote*
THURSDAY, AUGUST 28—*The Lead Up to Obama's Speech, Obama's Speech*
FRIDAY, AUGUST 29—*DNC Meeting*
SATURDAY, AUGUST 30—*Reflections on the Convention*

Chapter Three

93 *The General Election—Will He Make It?*

FIVE CONCERNS
MCCAIN PLAYS THE PATRIOT, POW, MAVERICK AND LOVE OF COUNTRY CARDS
REFLECTIONS FROM GEORGIA ON THE OBAMA CAMPAIGN

Chapter Four

109 *Obama, Thank God! Election Day, November 4, 2008*

MORE THOUGHTS ABOUT THE SOUTH
ELECTION DAY MORNING
ELECTION DAY AFTERNOON
ELECTION DAY EVENING
ELECTION DAY RESULTS

Chapter Five

129 *A Week to be Remembered: January 14-21, 2009*

JANUARY 14-16: MEETINGS WITH SEVERAL GROUPS IN NEW YORK CITY
JANUARY 17-18: NAACP AND CHURCH MEETINGS

JANUARY 19: THE BROOKLYN STEPPERS
JANUARY 20: BEFORE THE SWEARING IN
JANUARY 20: THE SWEARING IN
JANUARY 21: NATIONAL PRAYER SERVICE
JANUARY 21: THE CHANGE OF LEADERSHIP AT THE DNC

169 *Appendices*

JANUARY 14, 2009 SPEECH TO THE ENVIRONMENT
PROTECTION AGENCY (EXCERPTS)
OPEN LETTER TO THE BLACK PRESS

Acknowledgments

THERE ARE SO MANY PEOPLE WHO DESERVE MY GRATITUDE THAT IT would require another volume to thank them all.

So I will confine myself to family, staff, and parishioners. I am so dependent on my family for any meaningful undertaking that I cannot entertain a thought, to say nothing of an action, without their participation; in fact, it is true for all our family members. The extraordinary achievement of each member of the family is the achievement of and for all. Karen, Leah, Sharon, Dawn, Herb Jr., Lorenzo have all contributed so much in so many ways.

I want to thank Ayana Vincent, who, during the time she worked with us, spent considerable time working with me on this manuscript.

Also, Jerry King, for providing invaluable research assistance. I have no words to adequately express my gratitude to Chyann Starks. This brilliant, energetic, industrious, dependable, then a high school senior, spent endless hours including school breaks, helping with the editorial work and interacting with the publisher.

To all of my parishioners of The House of the Lord Church. I am eternally grateful for their comprehensive support and encouragement, and for always giving me the freedom to be and act according to my understanding of God's will for my life -- which often departed from the conventional and the traditional.

And to God be the glory, through Jesus Christ, my Lord and Savior, who counted me, chief of among sinners, worthy enough to save and call to The Ministry, giving me the opportunity to incorporate innumerable others in the noblest of missions: to heal, to help, and to save the human family. And so, now nearing octogenarian status, I can truthfully say, there may be some people who feel as grateful, honored, happy, and fulfilled as I do, but none feel more as I do.

Introduction

BY AND LARGE, THIS BOOK IS COMPRISED OF ARTICLES I WROTE FOR the *Daily Challenge*, a news publication disseminated primarily in the New York City metropolitan area. Its publisher is Thomas Watkins Jr.

Sometimes, when an author is reviewing articles written months or years ago, with the purpose of writing a book, he or she discovers references that are inconsistent with historical facts. Perhaps the author's opinions have changed—and mortals do change their minds. Perhaps the person written about has changed—and mortals do change. Does the author now make the changes that are consistent with reality at the time of the book's formation? Or does the author "let it all hang out," mistakes, miscalculations, misinterpretations, and inaccuracies? It is not an easy decision to make.

Who is eager to say, "I made a mistake. My facts are inaccurate" or "I'm sorry, I portrayed you falsely." In this book, I've chosen to let things stand as they were originally written. I would rather admit error and/or misrepresentation than alter history. I yield to the scriptural admonition (with modification): "Let God be true and every man a liar." I say, "Let history be true and every writer a liar."

Facing unyielding history is not all bad or terrifying; much can be gained from a reading or study of history, with all its truths and errors, highs and lows, wisdom and folly, compassion and cruelty, love and hate; with all of its contradictions, complexities, and inconsistencies. Each generation, given the truth of the preceding generation, has the option of improving or repeating. So, dear reader, what you have in your hands is what was written at a given time in the past. The dates of these writings have been put on the articles for all to see. Take the truth for what it is, the good and the bad, the accuracies and inaccuracies, the beautiful and the ugly.

There are two other decisions I had to make: *repetition* and *digression*. Repetition is inevitable when writing newspaper columns for a long period of time. As I previously noted about the changing of history, the same is true regarding repetition. Should the repetition be removed? I decided to keep the repetition just as it was written in the original articles. To remove or delete the repetition would be an alteration of history. What was written at the time was written for a reason. To delete would be to change something and therefore tamper with the integrity of the event.

Moreover, repetition is not necessarily a bad thing. Witness advertising companies spending millions, repeating their slogans as they attempt to sell their products. Mind doctors tell us that repetition is one way to fix an idea in our minds and create new habits.

Regarding digressions, as I write I think of other events and personalities that have been a part of my life that, in some way, connect to the subject matter before me. Then I feel compelled to make the connection. I hope the inclusion will expand the reservoir of knowledge and understanding.

In the same vein, I am often driven to be didactic or moralistic. Let the reader be patient and remember I am a minister of the gospel of Jesus Christ.

Writing about the 2008 campaign for the presidency of the United States was a towering, exhilarating challenge during a pivotal time in American history. Here we had an African American, and a woman candidate, locked in a bitter rivalry for the leadership for one of America's major political parties.

To further complicate the task, there was no absolute right and no absolute wrong. There were no cowboys (as in B-movies), good guys in white hats and suits, bad guys in black hats and suits. On both sides, this campaign was fraught with lies, truths, misrepresentations, contradictions, confusion, charges and countercharges, and name-calling. To sum it up, there were highs and lows, light and darkness, truth and error, consideration and inconsideration, all of which threatened to fragment the Democratic Party. And it was happening among old friends, allies, and veterans of the party.

And so we found ourselves with the deep agony of choosing sides. The words of Jesus, predicting the fragmentation his message would bring among family and friends, were painfully applicable to the Clinton/Obama quest for the Presidency of the United States of America. I witnessed and participated in heated arguments. I saw and heard of families and old friends engaging in verbal wars—which sometimes came close to physical violence over the candidates.

Personally, it was one of the most agonizing times in my life. Here was one of the epochal moments of history—a moment that, relatively speaking, comes to few in their lifetime. And, even more, here was the opportunity to participate in history and yet, I was on the sidelines.

This was a decision I made based upon my daughter Leah's position as Chief of Staff of the Democratic National Committee, and CEO of the Democratic National Convention, which demanded neutrality. But I would still be in a deep dilemma even if the neutrality of my daughter's position was not demanded. I know I speak for many African Americans when I say I knew a little about the Clintons and appreciated what they had done for African Americans. I also believed I knew what Mrs. Clinton would do if she were elected president; compared to Obama, whom I didn't know, and I didn't know many people who knew him well. And I was uncertain what he had done and what he would do if elected. But he was an African American, a kinsman, bone of my bone, flesh of my flesh. If there were no Leah, I would still be left trying to make a decision. Honesty compels me to say, I was not sure who would do the most, concretely, for African Americans.

As the campaign heated up and Obama's chances of winning became increasingly possible, I was asked what my choice was daily. In February, after Super Tuesday, arguments intensified around family dinner tables, in restaurants, school rooms, community rallies, and yes, even in churches and masjids (mosques). Everybody, it seemed, was digging in and doing battle.

In a March 11, 2008 *Daily Challenge* article, A. Peter Bailey, who edited Malcolm X's newsletter, identified six black categories/perspectives of blacks on the Obama campaign:

1. **The African Americans** who believed that the nation would really elect a black president. This group, he said, included many young black folk who rarely experienced overt racism and were often totally unaware of Jesse Jackson's 1984 run in the Democratic primary.

2. **African Americans** who supported Obama because of his symbolic value. Win or lose they believed that the campaign was important especially for the youth.

3. **African Americans** who supported Obama because he is black.

4. African Americans, primarily seniors, who have vivid recollection of the brutality of white racists against "uppity blacks." Although they supported Obama emotionally, they didn't want to see him elected because they feared he would be assassinated.

5. African Americans who happen-to-be-black and will not support Obama because he is black. This group believes whites were/are and will always be in charge. So fixed are they in their belief that they have no use for blacks who challenge them.

6. African Americans, a small group of blacks, who want Obama to be the Democratic candidate because he is the perfect one, not too dark, Harvard educated, not too threatening—to prove their point that voters in this country will not elect a black man as President in the foreseeable future. Once that is established, such people may see the necessity of organizing a sophisticated solution-oriented, black-led political movement, not tied to the Democrats or Republicans. Thus, they would be in a position to negotiate with either party on any given issue deemed important in promoting and protecting black economic, political, and cultural interest.

The arguments were good in the sense that everybody was passionately involved. This had positive potential far into the future. On the other hand, it was bad for the obvious reasons. "It was tearing us apart." In some instances, I wondered if reconciliation would ever be effectuated. It goes without saying that the altercations occurred during the primaries, but during the general election black people were almost 100% for Obama.

Onto this battlefield, I bravely (or foolishly) ventured. I tried to bring clarity, balance, fairness, information, and interpretation, while maintaining neutrality as much as humanly possible. I was compelled to do this, not only for others, but also for myself. I wrote an article (included in Chapter One) entitled, "Clinton or

Obama: Which Way Black America?" I tried to persuade African Americans that whichever side was chosen, we should believe that the decision was made from a sincere conviction that the candidate selected was the better for African Americans. I was hit from both sides, reminding me of a saying I heard somewhere, "If you try to walk in the middle of the road, you might get hit from both sides."

Added to my agony was my awareness that whatever I wrote—in fact, whatever I said or did—might have consequences on my daughter's position and future. The last thing I wanted to do was add more stress to her life. Daily, in myriad situations, I found myself walking a tightrope, constantly asking myself, "How will this affect Leah?"

I had 50 years of struggle, I reasoned. I had about reached my zenith (maybe already passed it). Now it was her time—my children's time, the next generation's time. She must carry on the family tradition. In our family, we believe that we have a covenant with God. If we live right, struggle with and for the people, God will bless our lives with meaning and purpose. Now it was Leah's time and I felt it was my duty to support her. I was gladly willing to let her increase while I decreased.

I humbly offer this book, which is my maximum effort to understand, analyze, and interpret, while fairly and truthfully presenting what was an exciting, tension-packed, ever-changing, and unprecedented political campaign for the most powerful position in the world. I am hopeful that it will educate, inspire, and motivate, thusly, adding to the library of human knowledge in some small way. Toward that end, even if my failings appear stark and embarrassing, I will be satisfied.

To underscore, I have dealt with moving, life-changing reality—not static, distant, dead reality. Writing a daily column or a running account of events is an attempt to capture contemporary reality. Surely, history is employed, but history is not the major player; it is a supporting actor. The heading of my column sums it up, "Writing the History I've Lived, Living the History I Write!"

Finally, I'm eternally gratefully that God has allowed me—who had been a destructive force in my youth and who has been an imperfect servant—to live to see it all. I am thankful to have made a tiny contribution, and to have recorded a small piece of it.

I have summed up the essence of life, or our reason for being, with three challenges:

To make history—that is, to contribute to the good of the human family.

To interpret history—that is, to help understand what is happening and one's own involvement.

To record history—that is, to leave a record of what has happened, even if it's only a diary or a journal.

To God be the glory, I've been blessed to do all three.

In My Lifetime

CHAPTER ONE

Super Tuesday to the End of the Democratic Primaries: February 2008-June 2008

Daily Challenge
WEEKEND EDITION, FEBRUARY 8-10, 2008

SUPER TUESDAY

SUPER TUESDAY IS OVER. I WATCHED THE PROCEEDINGS INTO the morning. My eyes were on the TV, but my mind was elsewhere. I could not tear my thoughts away from Georgia. Georgia was the first state to report a winner in Super Tuesday: Barack Obama. Those of us who grew up in Georgia—in the South in general—when old Jim Crow ruled the southland, must have wondered if we were dreaming. Perhaps Obama's win in South Carolina might have confirmed that we were experiencing reality. But to win in Georgia is another question. Georgia was the state of "Colored Only" signs, seemingly implacable discrimination; denial to blacks of any opportunity or decency; bombings, lynching, and unspeakable cruelties to blacks.

When I grew up in Savannah and Augusta, Georgia, our mothers and fathers would have settled for decent treatment. Most of them had forced themselves to adjust to segregation. It may be hard for those who never experienced the unbridled hatred, dehumanizing systems and unspeakable cruelty of the old South, to understand why those of us who lived in the belly of the beast, rejoice in what might seem to others as modest progress.

Did a black man really win in Georgia or was I dreaming?

The event becomes even more surreal when I looked at the voter breakdown; Obama won 39% of the white vote to Hillary's 57%; white men gave Obama 46% to Hillary's 49%; white women Hillary 62% to Obama's 36%.

Of Whites between the ages of 18-29, 77% went for Obama; so did whites ages 33-44, 74%. Did anybody in Georgia ever believe that 46% of white men would vote for a black candidate for Presidency of the United States? Or in the age category of 18-44, the support for Obama would be over 77%?

It is true that Jesse Jackson won South Carolina in the '84 and '88 elections. It was a major victory, make no mistake about it. It set the stage for Obama's success. Let us never forget that. We owe Jesse eternal gratitude for all that he has done, especially during his quest of the Presidency of the United States. The major difference between the campaigns of Obama and Jesse was/is the white participation. Obama won 25% of the white vote in South Carolina and 39% in Georgia. He won Iowa where there is a 95% white population.

Why were whites voting for Obama?

- His name? As whites looked at his name they might have thought he was white or a foreigner or from out of space, anything, anybody, but one of their "negras" or "uncles" or "boys." There used to be a joke "Making the Rounds" when I was young, maybe it really happened. The story is told of an African American who wanted equal service in the South. He would put on African apparel; whisper some mumble jumble that was supposed to be an African language, point to what he wanted or where he wanted to go. The subterfuge would work every time, to the gleeful satisfaction of the perpetrators. We would all get a big laugh out of the trickery.

- Guilt? Maybe whites wanted to do penance for their savage history or treatment to blacks. The scourge of conscience whipped them into the Barack camp.

- White Mama? They could identify and feel a part of Obama's campaign because of his white mama. They could blot out his black father. Some whites are good at negation. They taught us that "Columbus discovered America."

- A new day? Whites in the USA have really transcended race. The dream of Martin Luther King Jr. has become true even beyond the expectations of his dream. It is not just, "...a dream that one day on the red hills of Georgia, the sons of former slave owners will be able to sit down together at the table of brotherhood…" and that we are finally living in a society, "where we are not judged by the color of our skin but by the content of our character." Now in Georgia, white men and women, especially youth, have cast their ballot for a black man to become the President of the United States.

- Dislike for Hillary? Another reason is the antipathy for Hillary Clinton. Resentment for Mrs. Clinton has been expressed so strongly that it is conceivable that votes would be cast because of rejection of her.

The Bible teaches there is a time and season for every purpose under Heaven. Perhaps this is the time—starting or continuing with what has begun in the Obama campaign, that race no longer matters. Perhaps, the time has come, we can say to Dr. Cornel West "Race Does Not Matter." In the words of Victor Hugo perhaps, "it is an idea whose time has come" and in the words of Shakespeare's "Hamlet" "it is a consummation devoutly to be wished."

But we, who are the aged and aging ones, have seen our bright sunshine of hope die in the chill of betrayals and sell-outs. We thought we had turned the corner in 1865 with the end of the Civil War. The 13th, 14th, and 15th Amendments had freed the slaves, conferred citizenship and gave voter rights with representatives respectively. Thaddeus Stevens argued for legislation which would give former slaves land and resources; and the Freedmen's Bureau was created on March 4, 1865, which gave slaves land and resources. Yes, we thought that the nation was now ready to live up to its Creed and Pronouncements.

In 1865-1880 when the Civil War had ended expectations were high. Truly, black people's slave days were over. Black people had agitated for years on the evils of slavery, creating over 50 anti-slavery societies. The country, it seemed had come to accept that position. Black people had fought on the behalf of the Union. In fact, it was said that there would have been no Union without the black soldiers; the South would have won the war. Abraham Lincoln said as much.

So, there was great anticipation. The days of bondage were over. Freedom and justice had begun. Long live the Union! Political gain enhanced the hope still more. Legislatures of the South had ample black representation; from the state of Mississippi came two black U.S. Senators, Hiram R. Revels and Blanche K. Bruce. In 1866, Congress passed the Civil Rights bill over the veto of President Andrew Johnson. In 1875, more Civil Rights laws were enacted, and there were the constitutional safeguards as I have stated, in the 13th, 14th and 15th Amendments.

But the rosy picture was soon shattered. The hooded racists of the South began to ride, spreading terror, death and destruction. (That's why black people are not frightened by bin Laden or terrorists. We have been living with terror from the day they haunted us, captured and enslaved us up to the present time. And, incredibly this terror to which we have been subjected had often emanated from the law enforcement apparatus.) By the turn of the century, the nation had experienced another radical change, and the high hopes ushered in with termination of the Civil War were dashed to the ground. The road the country had decided to take with the election of Rutherford B. Hayes in 1876 was quite clear. A compromise was struck wherein the white South agreed to the election of the aforementioned pusillanimous President, in exchange for which they would regain their autonomy, and that meant that blacks would be theirs to do with as they pleased. And they were pleased to bomb and lynch black people into a state of servile submission.

By the way, it is interesting to note that in the South Carolina Constitutional Convention held January 14, 1868, of the 124 delegates 78 were black and of that number 13 were ministers, about one-sixth of the total. And it was a black minister,

Richard H. Cain, who was elected to be one of the state's four Congressmen. So around 140 years later, two black persons win South Carolina in their attempts to become President of the United States of America. Should black people be excited for what we have called the success of Jesse and Obama 140 years later?

So, we are not dreaming. Obama did win Georgia. But are whites really genuine and serious this time? For those of us who, like Bishop Desmond Tutu in South Africa, are addicted to hope, let us hope and pray this change is real, sincere, and permanent. And indeed the last part of King's dream would have been realized when "...all God's children, black men, white men, Jews and Gentiles, Protestants and Catholics, will be able to join hands and sing in the words of the old Negro spiritual: "*Free at last! Free at last! Thank God Almighty, we are free at last!*"

Daily Challenge WEDNESDAY, FEBRUARY 20, 2008

OBAMA OR CLINTON: WHICH WAY BLACK AMERICA?

BEFORE I ADDRESS THE QUESTION, OBAMA/CLINTON: WHICH way Black America? I cannot help touching on Obama's sweep on the weekend of February 9, 2008. He won all the states: Washington, Nebraska, Maine, the Virgin Islands, and Louisiana. Louisiana was kind of expected, but the other states? Who would have thought it a few months ago? Increasingly, the possibility of Obama becoming the Democratic Party Standard Bearer looms large and his becoming President of the United States is now within the realm of possibility.

Still, there is a question which I ponder often. Which candidate would better serve the USA and in particular the interest of African Americans—Senator Hillary Clinton or Senator Barack Obama? Symbolically there is no contest. Obviously, it is Obama. We should not dismiss or minimize the importance of symbols. There is a quote from Paul Tillich, a renowned theologian, on symbols. This quote, which Dr. King cited in his 1955 doctoral dissertation, was said to have been taken from the dissertation written by Dr. Jack Boozer three years earlier. Dr. Boozer, like Dr. King, was a graduate student from Boston University. Here is the quote: "Tillich insists that a symbol possesses a necessary character. It cannot be exchanged. A sign, on the contrary, is impotent and can be exchanged at will. A religious symbol is not the creation of a subjective desire or work. If the symbol loses its ontological grounding, it declines and becomes a mere 'thing,' a sign impotent in itself."

Obama's very presence, to say nothing of his success in the presidential race, has inspired unnumbered blacks, minorities, young people, indeed all people of decency and fairness. For my purpose, I want to focus on people of African ancestry. Wherever I've gone, Africa in particular, there is a glowing pride when his name is mentioned. Moreover, if Obama should win, only God knows how far-reaching the impact. For those who have been so inspired will surely make their mark on the world and history.

However, beyond symbolism and all that means, the question still remains, who would benefit African Americans the most in terms of jobs or positions, businesses and or economic opportunities, allocation or direction of resources to the black communities, appointments to important offices (which blacks have not held before), health care, affirmative action, reparations, education, assistance for African countries and third world countries in general? In other words, at the conclusion of his or her future, who would have benefited African Americans the most?

When I size up the candidates, this is what looks me in the face: Senator Hillary Clinton.

Personally, I have interacted with the Clintons in various ways. In 1992, I did the invocation at the Democratic Executive Committee meeting. This meeting happens after the Convention has selected its Presidential candidates. All the Democratic bigwigs assembled there, including the nominees, President and Vice President, Clinton and Gore, respectively.

During Clinton's presidency, I used to be one of the relatively few ministers invited periodically to the White House for interracial, interfaith clergy breakfasts. There were other functions in Washington, D.C. and the community involving the Clintons in which I participated. I was at the White House for a reception for Nelson Mandela on his last visit to the United States during the Clinton administration.

Moreover, during the Clinton years, my daughter, Leah, who interned at Congressman Ed Towns' office during her sophomore year at Dartmouth College, upon graduating in 1984, went to work full time for the Congressman. From there, she went to the Democratic National Committee (DNC), when Mr. Ron Brown was chairperson. Brown then sent Leah to New York City to make preparations for the 1992 Democratic Convention. After which, she went to work at the Labor Department as Special Assistant to Ms. Alexis Herman, who was Secretary of Labor. She was eventually appointed Chief of Staff of the DNC by Mr. Terry McAuliffe, which position she still holds. Several months ago, she was appointed by Howard Dean, the current Chairperson of the DNC, to Chief Executive Officer (CEO) of the Democratic National Convention, which will take place in August 2008 in Denver, Colorado.

There were other appointments of significance for blacks that I knew and many others that I did not know. There were other gains which blacks achieved during the Clinton years.

I think every black person knew someone who knew someone who knew the Clintons. While a lot of us wouldn't go as far as Toni Morrison, to call Bill Clinton the first black president, and 99 9/10% of us surely would vigorously disagree with Obama's rejection of Clinton as a black president because he couldn't dance, but, I think overall, a fair assessment of Clinton's relationship to blacks has been better than good and far better than other presidents.

In addition, blacks in particular that I have known for years are high in Mrs. Clintons' campaign staff and are among her top advisors. They and others speak highly of Mrs. Clinton.

SENATOR BARACK OBAMA

When I consider Obama there is nothing to consider. I don't know him. I met him once in passing at the Democratic National Convention in Boston, 2004. I liked him then; I like him now. I don't know what he has done for Black people in his community or in his law practice. I don't know anyone around him or close to him who is advising him. Now, the above doesn't mean that Obama is not Afro-centric. Maybe he realizes if he is going to win the Presidential campaign, he will have to have the support of whites. Therefore, he cannot be too black or black at all. What he or Mrs. Clinton will do once he or she is elected, who knows?

Well, there is the dilemma for those of us who are Afrocentric and have had dealings with the Clintons and none with Obama. So, when we see conscious black people supporting Mrs. Clinton, we ought to be understanding and respectful of their decisions although we disagree. Let us believe that they probably arrived at their decision after soul searching and that it is not loyalty alone that drives their decision for Clinton. They sincerely believe Mrs. Clinton is the best choice for Americans and African Americans in particular.

Just as for those who support Mr. Obama ought not to be

labeled naïve or "color consumed," rather let us ascribe to them a thoughtful process which moved them to favor Sen. Obama while surely race placed a part but it was concern for the best interest of people of African ancestry that drove their decision.

For myself, I still agonize. There is another piece with which I wrestle. As aforementioned, my daughter Leah is the CEO of the Democratic National Committee. Her position demands neutrality. I believe anything I do that is newsworthy will reflect on her. Hence, I do not want to do anything that would subject her to questions of her loyalty to neutrality based upon decisions that I made. Therefore, I have decided to refrain from public endorsements. I am a father, who is in his 50th year of ministry. I have had my times. Now, I am blessed to have children to carry on the family tradition of working and struggling with and for the people. Leah is not only all of the above mentioned; she is also a pastor—the 5th generation of ministers in our family.

I conclude in the place where I started, or with the question I raised, Obama or Clinton—Which Way Black America? We can be grateful that we are living at a time that many of us thought would never come. Inevitably, the Democratic Party will have as its leader a person of African ancestry or a woman, and who knows, we might have both.

P.S. As I was completing this article, on the TV there were charges of plagiarism and the stealing of ideas by the Clinton and Obama camps. Clinton people claimed that Obama in a speech he made copied the words of Massachusetts Governor Deval Patrick who in his 2006 campaign speech said, "I have a dream'—just words? 'We hold these truths to be self-evident, that all men are created equal'—just words?" Obama admitted that he should have given credit to the Governor, but he shot back at Clinton accusing her of taking his words, "I'm fired up…" Both of them took my words, "Fired up…" which I popularized across the nation in the '70s and '80's. I first heard these words in South Carolina at a demonstration to free Ben Chavis, who was a member of the Wilmington 10. They were accused of rioting and unlawful acts. The demonstrators used the words, "I'm fired up, can't take no more!" I changed the words to "Fired up, won't take no more!" which places a different interpretation of the words.

DAILY CHALLENGE THURSDAY, FEBRUARY 28, 2008

ALAS POOR HILLARY, THE MYSTERIES ARE AGAINST THEE!

IT IS 5:09 AM, FEBRUARY 13TH, I HAD BEEN UP SINCE 2:30 AM, writing, researching, filing and preparing for tomorrow's or today's obligations, all the while I watched CNN report on the Potomac Primary—Virginia, Washington, DC, and Maryland. I started watching at 8:30 pm the night before. Everybody knows Senator Obama won big time. Equally impressive is the source of his victory. In Super Tuesday he won 57% of the youth, last night he won 68%. Super Tuesday 35% of the 65+ year olds, last night he won 51%. He won 59% last night over against 35% of the rural vote. Super Tuesday he won 47% of Latino vote to 53% in the Potomac Primaries. What this represents is a steady increase from groups that had been in Senator Clinton's camp or who had not been Senator Obama's supporters. He beat Hillary in the Latino community in Virginia; also he won the women's vote, both strongholds of Clinton's campaign.

This must cause great concern among Mrs. Clinton's supporters. Youth, college educated, independent, blacks and white males have been Obama's base. He is growing stronger in his base even while making inroads into Mrs. Clinton's base of support.

Another consideration that must worry the Clintons—Senator Obama is winning the Caucus states. This means skillful, tedious organizing. It takes a well-run organization to win Caucus states. In other words, Senator Obama is out-organizing Senator Clinton. It is reported he has spent a lot of money on grassroots or base organizing. On the question of money, he has raised substantially more cash than Mrs. Clinton. So, the Democratic nomination for Mrs. Clinton doesn't seem promising.

I really feel compassion for Mrs. Clinton. At times, she appears confused and/or stunned—like suddenly being hit by an unexpected blow or like a deer staring into the bright lights of an oncoming car. After New Hampshire, she said, "You helped me to find my voice," but as the campaign progressed she must have lost her voice again. Top staff people have been fired. It seems she has inherited all her husband's enemies and few of his friends. Also, for Mr. Clinton, my feelings go out to him. He has tried so hard—too hard, some would say—to help his wife, and the media have not been kind to him.

Studying the campaigns, it seems there are two indefinable things that are against Senator Clinton—momentum and destiny. Maybe they are the same. There is a mystery about them. They just seem to happen or they seem to have minds of their own. Mysteriously they appear and mysteriously they disappear. Those of us who have played or watched some form of sports, know about momentum. We call it the "mighty mo." When it shows up you feel carried along. You can't lose. Similarly, it also happens with destiny. When they are on your side, your opponents don't stand a chance. A bad bounce that helps you or hinders the opposition, or a miracle play occurs. Consider, for example, the catch made by David Tyree. After Eli Manning had miraculously eluded huge linemen, he threw a pass downfield. David, with an opposing player hanging on his back, caught the ball with one hand holding it against his helmet as he fell to the ground. Somehow, the ball never hit the ground. This miracle catch, in the waning seconds of the game, enabled the New York Giants to beat the highly favored New England Patriots in the 2008 Super Bowl Game. Or remember the catch by Willie Mays in the 1954 World Series when the New York Giants beat the Cleveland Indians.

Momentum reminds me of two body motions, metabolism the breaking down and building up of the body, and peristalsis: the wavelike action in the colon that enables elimination of waste from the body. There is a lot of mystery around these two motions. They just seem to have always been there and without conscious effort, they just happen. Our health depends upon how well they function. Some health specialists have argued that all illness has its origin in the colon. So, momentum comes and goes like the wind. As of this writing, Senator Obama has the "mighty mo" on his side. How long? Who knows?

Also he has destiny smiling upon him. Things just seem to be going his way. He is a miracle man. Who can explain him? At this point, he is the "idea whose time has come." But, who or what makes the idea come at a certain time in history? Some people say destiny is just another way of saying God, for people who, for whatever reason, don't want to bring God into the game or subject, surely not into a political campaign.

Consider how strange and miraculous are the man and his campaign. A few months ago, most people didn't know who he was. Mrs. Clinton was a sure winner. She had "all the toys in the sandbox," money, connection, experience, etc. It was thought that by Super Tuesday, it would be all over. The Democratic Party, with its standard bearer, Mrs. Clinton, would have months to strategize and fund raise in preparation for the General Election. Then something happened on the way to the coronation. Along comes this relatively young black man with a funny name, unknown, or little known, with limited connections and money. He was dismissed by some pundits, or the people who are supposed to know, as an object of laughter and ridicule. And now at this writing, he has defeated Mrs. Clinton in 10 states. He has passed her in delegates. He has raised more money and is better organized and he has "mighty mo" going for him. These developments now have pundits, former critics and naysayers, declaring Mr. Obama the winner to become the Democratic candidate for President of the United States. Further, there are polls declaring him to be the winner if John McCain is the Republican nominee. Could anybody imagine or dream or give time to the thought a few months ago—in fact even now—that a Black man, a relatively unknown one at that, would be the Democratic candidate and would be a favorite to win the Office of the President of the United States of America?

A few months ago had we verbalized such a thing, we would have been dismissed as irrational, ridiculed as stupid or condescendingly winked upon as naïve; but wonder of wonders, miracle of miracles, here we are! Here he is! And it's real! How can it be explained? Let the wise in these matters attempt to give a logical answer. Let the astute pundits provide a rational reason. Let others call it destiny, but when all is said and done their answers for me will not be sufficient.

Call me naïve, call me overly religious, call me what you will, but it is only with reference to God, that I can understand these strange and mysterious developments. According to the Bible, "God's ways are past finding out."

If I am right about momentum and God—maybe momentum is initiated by God as is metabolism and peristalsis and the action of the sinus node, that fires the action that influences the rhythm of the heart; I say, if I am right, and I'm not sure if I want to be right (I have great admiration for the Clintons, I believe they are good and have done a lot of good for black people in particular and the country in general), but if I am right, then it is written in the stars and the game is over. Forces beyond the control of either candidate are in charge. "The moving finger writes and having writ moves on. Neither words, nor wit, nor tears can lure back, or make it change or cancel one line of it," to paraphrase the fatalism of an Arabian writer.

Alas, poor Hillary, it wasn't meant to be unless, something miraculous should happen. Let me conclude with two other sports events. The first is the Immaculate Reception, in the championship game between the Oakland Raiders and Pittsburgh Steelers on December 23, 1972. Franco Harris caught a pass into his arms that bounced off a Dallas player named Jack Tatum while he was in full stride. He dashed across the goal line as the time on the clock ran out. That is why the play is called the Immaculate Reception. The other reference is to Doug Flutie of Boston College. On November 23, 1984, Boston College was behind the heavily favorite, unbeaten Miami Hurricanes. There was time for only one play. Flutie heaved a long pass into the Miami end zone. It ended up in the arms of a Boston player as the gun sounded ending the game. Flutie's throw was named the "Hail Mary Pass."

Maybe, there is a Hail Mary or an Immaculate Reception in Mrs. Clinton's playbook. Maybe, something will persuade the Mysteries to change their minds. God has been known to change his mind. In fact, recently, I preached a sermon on a King who was told by a Prophet to put his house in order for death awaited him. But after fervent and intense prayer, God added 15 years to the King's life. I don't know if there are praying people in the Clinton's camp; if there are, they had better hurry and get in touch with the Almighty.

P.S. As of this writing, 2/20/08, Senator Obama has just won Wisconsin and Hawaii. The pundits are having a field day exhausting their vocabularies, employing similes, metaphors, analogies, describing Obama's victory. John Roberts of

CNN said, "If they were playing nine ball in a pool game the game would be over." "He, Obama, keeps rolling along," said Larry King, CNN. "Huge momentum for Obama" Wolfe Blitzer, CNN

March 4th Primary, Texas and Ohio are must wins for Senator Clinton, even her husband the former President, Bill Clinton, said, "If she doesn't win those states, its all over for her." There are those who have already written Mrs. Clinton's political obituary. Still others say she has to not only win, but she must win big.

May 31, 2008 (Article did not appear in the *Daily Challenge*)

SHOWDOWN AT THE RULES AND BYLAWS COMMITTEE MEETING

PICKET SIGNS AND DEMONSTRATORS SURROUNDED THE WARDman Park Marriott Hotel in Washington, DC. Mrs. Clinton's supporters seemed to be in the overwhelming majority and they were loud. If vocal cords, signs and banners, and demonstrators were the criteria for victory, Mrs. Clinton would win going away.

Inside the hotel, they were still the majority. With Clinton buttons on and creative hats and apparel, they moved in groups throughout the first-floor area. They were conspicuous and noisy. Obama's people were less boisterous and conspicuous. You could feel their presence more than see it.

This meeting of the Rules and Bylaws Committee of the Democratic National Committee was one of the most important in the party's history. Unless they could resolve the conflict regarding Michigan and Florida, the party could be fractured beyond repair, rendering it powerless to win the general election. The bone of contention was Michigan and Florida's rejection of the party's rule regarding when primaries could be held. Michigan and Florida wanted their primaries pushed up before February 5th to "break the lock New Hampshire has had on the Presidential nominating process."

Michigan had started lobbying as far back as January 19, 2002, when Senator Carl Levin testified before the DNC and asked for a rule change in the Presidential nominating process. The DNC unanimously voted him down. They continued their efforts and as already stated, even though rejected, they held their primary on January 15, 2008, anyway. Meanwhile, the Republican-controlled Florida legislature insisted that Florida's Democrats move the date of the state-run primary from the 1st Tuesday of March (March 4, 2008) to January 29, 2008. (This put Florida in a different category than Michigan and further complicated the situation, making the Rules and Bylaws Committee's task even more difficult.)

In spite of the DNC warning that if they violated the rules, their delegates would be forfeited, as stated above, Michigan and Florida went ahead with their primaries. Mrs. Clinton won both states. Senator Obama, along with Senator John Edwards and Governor Bill Richardson, took their names off the ballot in Michigan in order to obey a pledge they had made not to campaign in states that were breaking DNC rules. Senator Clinton took the same pledge, but declined to reinforce the pledge and did not remove her name. So the meeting today, after months of bitter, vitriolic, and sometimes personal attacks, was for the Rules and Bylaws Committee to find a solution.

I was invited to attend the meeting. I had occasion to converse with many of the Rules and Bylaws Committee members. The tension was thick. Everybody seemed to be whispering. During lunch, members at the table where I sat tried to interject other subjects. It was like a game. Various topics were touched on lightly. There was joking and laughter, but it was all superficial. Everybody knew what was on everybody's mind. Victory or defeat in the general election, and the perpetuation of the Democratic Party now rested on their decision. Also, how the decision would be received primarily by Democratic Party members was equally as important.

After lunch, committee members went into a closed section. Hours later, they slowly returned to their places. They seemed reluctant to start the meeting. Some showed signs of exhaustion and frustration. There were others who seemed energized and excited. Just before the meeting resumed, I went over to greet the committee members while they stood around their seats. I tried to discern their decisions. I talked to one member who was reported to be an Obama supporter. We discussed the compromise that would be offered, not the results. The person looked at me, winked, nodded, and whispered, "We got this. Everything is under control." I think the person meant that the compromise was a done deal. And because of the rumor that this was an Obama supporter, I gathered that the decision would be favorable to Obama.

When I returned to my seat, a few feet to the side and back, I overheard three of Obama's people. They were talking softly to a fourth person. They were discussing the coming Tuesday night's primary election. They were saying there would be a major rally in Minnesota, after which there would be a party. They had counted the delegates and were now ascertaining a count for the after party. I knew then that the compromise would be favorable to Obama and that they had enough delegates to guarantee victory in the primary. I wondered what Clinton and her supporters would do when the compromise was announced. Would there be a party split? What is going to happen at the Convention? Would the opponents ever heal or be reconciled?

After heated debate by supporters of both candidates, it was time to vote. At 6:50 pm, by a vote of 27-0, with one abstention, the committee passed a proposal to seat all of Florida's delegates, giving each one only a half a vote. Mr. Harold Ickes, a long-time Democratic Party power player, expressed his disappointment that the delegates from the Sunshine State did not receive full voting rights, but supported the motion. At 7:15 pm, the Rules and Bylaws Committee voted 19-8 to approve a motion to restore all pledged delegates in Michigan, provided that each would be entitled to cast only one half vote. This would leave Mrs. Clinton with 69 delegates casting 34.5 votes. And Mr. Obama with 59 delegates casting 29.5 votes. Mr. Ickes again, but with greater anger said, "This body of 30 individuals has decided that they're going to substitute their judgment for 600,000 voters" (referring to the Michigan voters). He continued sarcastically, "Now that's what I call democracy." Significantly, the Florida/Michigan decisions by the committee changed the delegate count necessary to secure the party's nomination. It was originally 2,026. The new number now, according to the DNC was 2,118.

All during the debate, there were attempts to disrupt the proceedings. Many times, the gavel had to be hammered down by co-chairs, Mrs. Alexis Herman and Mr. James Roosevelt Jr., the grandson of President Franklin D. Roosevelt. Later, the disgruntled crowd, 90% white, took their screaming and stomping into the reception area of the hotel. They were followed by a horde of media people. They shouted, "Denver! Denver! Denver!" Meaning they would get even in Denver. I wondered, what form, or reaction, getting even in Denver would take? Would there be a floor fight? Would they splinter the party if they didn't get what they wanted? I was profoundly concerned.

Additionally, observing the drama throughout the day was agonizing for me. Most of the people with whom I had close associations, were in Hillary's camp. Their faces and body language showed pain, frustration, and anger. I wanted Mrs. Clinton to win, but I didn't want Obama to lose. I wanted Obama to win, but I didn't want Mrs. Clinton to lose. I wished there were a Co-Presidency. Then there would be no losers. Everybody would win. But... maybe nobody would win.

I wondered if the disruption at the meeting and in the reception area by whites was racially driven? Was it really about stopping a black man? I wondered if it would be the same if Obama had a different complexion and nationality? I hoped that for all concern, that whatever the outcome, the participants would rise above self interest, personal resentments, and slights; in a word, I hoped they could rise above whatever negative thing might have happened in the past and unite for the good of all.

It wasn't a joyful ride home. And, sleep didn't come easily. I couldn't stop replaying the scenes of the day—seeing faces and hearing voices; at the same time, I was grateful that I had been present at one of the most important moments in Democratic Party history.

JUNE 2008 (ARTICLE DID NOT APPEAR
IN THE *Daily Challenge*)

THE PRIMARY ELECTION HEARD AROUND THE WORLD

IT WAS 9:30 PM WHEN WOLF BLITZER, CNN ANCHORMAN, AN-nounced Barack Obama had gained enough delegates to make him the winner of the Democratic Presidential nomination, while across the TV screen flashed "Breaking News."

My eyes and mind turned from my writing (from the comfort of my bed where I had retired early) and became fixed on the TV. I tried to absorb and savor the moment. I had difficulty grasping the reality. Was it real or was I dreaming? Was it true in my lifetime, the impossible had become possible? My mind raced backward to the early years of slavery. I could hear the voice of Rev. Henry Highland Garnet, "let your motto be resistance, resistance, resistance." Frederick Douglass, "Without struggle there is no progress." Dr. King, "I have a dream." It seemed I could feel the thunder of countless marching feet, the tension, conflict and jail cells; I could hear the explosion of bombs on homes and churches. The mourns of lynching, all of our 400 years of struggling and suffering—now finally we have reached where no black man had gone before and lead in the polls in the race for the Presidency of the United States of America.

For the hoary heads, stooped shoulders and bent backs, especially for those of us who were born and bred in the South who can still remember the dehumanizing system of segregation—this was unreal. Yet, somehow I could feel the cry of ecstasy. I knew it was beating in the heart of every person of African ancestry who had any race consciousness left, or who still had an ounce of self-respect. Irrespective of the political choice one had made, or whether one liked Obama or not, surely his victory, at this point, must be viewed as a victory for people of African ancestry the world over.

Yes, I remembered the negative things they were saying about him and the public criticisms too, but there he was: handsome, intelligent, articulate, knowledgeable, charismatic—a son of Africa and nobody could take his victory from him. Oh, they tried—Hillary and her people. There were subtle or more often than not blatant acts of denial and attempts to diminish Obama's triumph. When they grudgingly conceded Obama's victory it was always put in the context of Hillary's achievement, i.e., Hillary got 18 million votes (of course, if you count Michigan and Florida which shouldn't have been counted. After all, they broke the rules. And Hillary didn't start thinking about those votes until it became obvious that she had lost or was losing). They emphasized the states she had won as "must win states" to beat the Republicans. They emphasized her winning white blue collar workers, seniors and women, the people Democrats must win to get to the White House. The message was clear: Hillary ought to be the candidate. Governor Rendell of Pennsylvania expressed openly what others said softly and privately, "Hillary is the stronger candidate." He said that while affirming his support for Obama. This behavior, along with other acts along the campaign trail, fueled the animosity that increased as the campaign dragged on.

This animosity burst forth at the Rules and Bylaws Committee Saturday, May 31, 2008, at the Wardman Park Marriott Hotel in Washington, D.C. All during the debate there were rowdies attempting to disrupt the proceedings. Many times the gavel had to be hammered down by Co-Chairs Ms. Alexis Herman and Mr. James Roosevelt Jr., the grandson of President Franklin Roosevelt. When the votes were cast, which accepted a compromise, Board Member Harold Ickes led the charge of the disgruntled board members. He said, "This is not the path to unity." Later the rowdies, 90% white, took to the reception area of the hotel and continued screaming and stomping, "Denver! Denver! Denver!" Meaning they will get even in Denver. Even during Hillary's speech they continued to shout, "Denver! Denver! Denver!" Significantly, she made no attempt to stop them as she had made no effort to quell the resentment of Obama even as it steadily rose to levels that could rupture the Democratic Party.

Just before the meeting resumed, I overheard three of Obama's people, just a few feet away from where I was seated, talking softly to a fourth person. They were talking about the coming Tuesday night primary election. They were saying there would be a major rally in Minnesota, after which there would be a party. They were counting delegates and ascertaining a count for the after party.

When board members returned from their prolonged lunch, I went to the committee members' table where Donna Brazile stood. I had had lunch with the committee members earlier. We conversed about the compromise that would be offered. She looked at me, winked, nodded her head and whispered, "We got this. Everything is under control." I think she meant the compromise was a done deal.

I came away from the meeting knowing two things, Obama had enough delegates to win and there was going to be an angry reaction.

Never once from the lips of Hillary and supporters did I hear an unqualified recognition and support of Obama. I saw and heard on CNN Mr. Lanny Davis, an attorney and longtime Clinton supporter, who knew Hillary as a college student. After Obama had won, he immediately wrote a letter to the *New York Times* urging acceptance of Hillary as Vice President. Bob Johnson, BET founder and seller of same (you couldn't expect him to do otherwise) used the most offensive language with reference to Obama early in the campaign. He too wrote a letter to the Congressional Black Caucus urging them to endorse Hillary for Vice President. Governor Ed Rendell, his comments already cited; Mr. McAuliffe, campaign manager and longtime Clinton admirer and supporter, really said it all, "This is Hillary's night." Earlier, he had introduced Hillary as the next President of the United States of America. And then there was Charlie Rangel adding his voice to the detractors. I must say I was surprised to see Rangel in the crowd. In fairness to Rangel, the next day, Wednesday, June 11, he redeemed himself. He congratulated Obama on his victory. Then in reference to Mrs. Clinton, he underscored that the New York delegation had always supported her. And, in Rangelian phraseology, said, "We will be there with her till the end. But we thought the end was the end." By Thursday, Rangel had organized the New York delegation and categorically endorsed Obama and reiterated his thought "the end was the end." So while they engaged in minimizing Obama they were maximizing Mrs. Clinton. They were spoiling a page of history that belonged to Obama.

As I witnessed this parade of sour grapes, or "sore losers" or "Machiavellian politics" all through the night it lit a spark of disbelief. Slowly the spark turned into a flame of irritation that grew to a fire of resentment; by morning I was in a state of boiling anger and resentment. My respect for the diminishers was diminished, as they continued to diminish Obama.

They had engaged in a concerted strategy to diminish the brightness of one of the greatest moments in American history, maybe in the world. Let me emphasize, Obama's victory I believe was not just for people of African ancestry the world over, but for America in particular and the world in general. They were thieves. They were robbing Obama of all he represented of what he rightfully won by the rules he was asked to observe.

I became convinced the inability or unwillingness of Mrs. Clinton and her supporters would defeat or minimize her chance to become the Vice President, as well as the campaign to force Obama to tap her for Number 2. It would in fact do the opposite or would disqualify her. It seems to me that Hillary and her supporters had forced Obama into a dilemma. He has to reject her as VP; to do otherwise would make him appear weak at best, or abdicating to a Clinton takeover. Then he would have a mass resistance, defection, disillusionment or all of the above from his supporters. If he rejects her then there might be a reaction from Mrs. Clinton's supporters.

By their actions, one is driven to believe that they would not settle for Number 2, in fact Number 1 is what they are really after. They could not get it through the front door so they would try through the back. Joe Madison, a well-known popular African American radio personality, when asked about Hillary's chances of Obama appointing her VP said, "if he did, he better get a taster." Sadly, Hillary and her supporters' actions gave weight to their enemies' accusations—"the Clintons are cold and calculating and would do anything to win." Putting aside the mockery, antics, and exaggerations of Father Michael Pfleger characterization of Hillary, one wonders if his reference to white privilege having been enjoyed so long that you can't concede to blackness, except when conceding or giving or doing nice things from a position of power.

When Hillary finished her speech, Jeffrey Toobin, CNN pundit, blurted out, "What deranged narcissism!" Unanimously, all the pundits criticized Hillary's speech. They called it, "defiant, ungracious, self-promoting," etc. Surely, the Clintons in many ways have done some good things for African Americans, but that is the point, THEY HAVE DONE FOR US, which basically means, they are in the power position or enjoy the power of the giver. What Obama represents is a change in the power equation. The table has turned. He is the giver of good things—and can dispense bad things too. It's a new ball game. The question then is: can the Clintons play in the new game? At the point of this writing, their action and attitude seem to suggest to all but the die-hard Clintonians they are unable or unwilling to make the adjustment. I hope I am wrong. I hope they will play ball.

No, it wasn't Clinton's night, as McAuliffe wanted the world to believe. It was Obama's night! It was a night that most people, yes, even black people, didn't think would ever come. It is a night, I believe, especially America should have celebrated and extended unqualified congratulations. Here is a man who had surmounted many of the towering obstacles that confront almost all who seek to achieve significant goals or are just trying to do something worthwhile. Therefore, all people can be inspired by Obama's accomplishments. Especially for our youth, our children, Obama is a model that can be employed as a challenge and motivation.

And to think there was this parade of Prometheans trying to steal Obama's fire. The major difference of course, Prometheus tried to steal fire from the gods for the good of humankind. These contemporary Prometheans are trying to steal the fire for their own political agendas. This much I will say: some of them, maybe a few, I will give them the benefit of the doubt, they truly believe their shenanigans will work out for the good of the country—and of course for themselves. Be that as it may, they still elected to join the fire stealers. So, the end result for Obama and all who understand the moment is a denial of what is rightfully Obama's place in the sun.

By late Wednesday, some of Hillary's supporters were changing their tunes. Led by Congressman Rangel, they were now backing away from their earlier attitudes and statements. By Thursday, they were all singing a different tune. They were now saying Hillary's speech was a mistake. Not enough was extended toward Obama. So, at the American Jewish Public Affairs Committee on June 8th, she heaped praise on him.

Then they started backing away from their push for Hillary as VP. Mrs. Clinton's people issued a statement, stating that nobody speaks for Mrs. Clinton except Mrs. Clinton. The decision for the VP is Obama's alone. The Communications Director signed the statement. Wolf Blitzer said there was pressure by Hillary Clinton's supporters to desist from pushing for the VP.

In a short period of time, Hillary's people made two awful decisions that they had to change. This turn of events is the story of the failed Clinton campaign. There were so many mistakes, mistakes that were hard to understand. Clinton and her people were supposed to be experienced professionals. How could they say and do things that even a novice would shun. And let it be remembered that she started out 30% ahead. She had it all going for her: experience, money, political heavyweights, connections, and recognition. She was running against a non-entity, a relatively unknown and she lost and in the end was still blundering, disgracefully blundering. They had to show the world they had blundered by rushing in with correctives.

Then, it came as a bombshell. Breaking news announced: Hillary Clinton and Obama were meeting. It was Wednesday evening. Obama was addressing a huge rally in Virginia when the news broke across the TV screen. The whereabouts of the meeting was unknown. Later it was learned it was at Senator Dianne Feinstein's home in Washington, D.C.

By now, Mrs. Clinton was telling the world she would express support for Senator Obama and party unity in Washington, D.C. on Saturday, June 7th. The speech she delivered won unanimous approval. Again she was late, which detracted from the luster of her speech.

I was relieved and delighted for the change in attitude and behavior by Clinton and her supporters for two reasons. Firstly, I liked the Clintons. I think they are decent, caring human beings. They have been good to people of African ancestry—and good for the country. Secondly, had she continued as she was going I believe she would have split the Democratic Party and made a wreck of her political future.

P.S. In light of Senator Hillary Clinton's loss to Senator Barack Obama, my mind rehearsed the primary campaign. All along the way, I kept feeling that there was something strange, different or unusual about the campaign. There were others who felt similarly. Old pros—Senators Ted Kennedy, John Kerry, and Governor Bill Richardson—when referring to Obama used such mystic terms as "there is something going on out there"; "It reminded me of Jack Kennedy's campaign for president"; "It is profound." I had looked at the mistakes that were made. It was unbelievable. After the primary election, the campaign chairman Terry McAuliffe was asked why there were no Clinton campaign operations in the Super Tuesday states. His response was, he didn't know. They had the money and he didn't know why.

In an article that I wrote back on February 28, 2008, I tried to express my difficulty understanding the campaign. (See "Alas, Poor Hillary the Mysteries Are Against Thee!")

CHAPTER TWO

Inside the 2008 Democratic National Convention — Putting it All Together

AUTHOR'S NOTE: The following journal of my Convention week activities originally appeared in various editions of the Daily Challenge, published in September and October 2008.

FRIDAY, AUGUST 22
Convention Thoughts

IT WAS A NEAR PERFECT MORNING. THE BABY BLUE SKY HAD JUST a touch of whiteness. Dew was still on the soft green grass, the trees were tall and strong, as if standing guard over the neighborhood, while providing shade and lodging for chirping birds.

Sitting in the office of Councilman Charles Barron weeks

earlier, discussing projects that would enhance his district, he began to expound with childish glee about recently discovered lore on the importance of trees and their role in the overall betterment of the community. When he was finished, I said, "I have a greater appreciation of trees," and I began to mumble the poem "Trees" by Joyce Kilmer:

> *I think that I shall never see a poem lovely as a tree.*
> *A tree whose hungry mouth is pressed*
> *Against the earth's sweet flowing breast;*
> *A tree that looks at God all day,*
> *And lifts her leafy arms to pray,*
> *A tree that may in summer wear*
> *A nest of robins in her hair;*
> *Upon whose bosom snow has lain;*
> *Who intimately lives with rain.*
> *Poems are made by fools like me,*
> *But only God can make a tree.*

And I remembered a brother in a Trenton, New Jersey, prison who used to sing the poem with such feeling and rhythm that even the most incorrigible inmate was captivated.

The kaleidoscopic colors of blooming flowers added their special touch to the morning delight. I was reminded that I hadn't watered my plants on the stoop. The sprinkler system is designed to do its work every other day. But my flowers can't wait; they move to a rhythm that Mother Nature orchestrates.

So, as we were driving to the airport, we passed Hawthorne Elementary School, a one-story sprawling school set in a square block of expansive green grass with baseball and football fields. My mind raced back to the day I registered our son at Hawthorne. It was a small class, but what struck me was that there was a red carpet on the floor. As if tuned into my reverie, my driver, a Jordanian said, "My son went to that school," nodding towards Hawthorne. "Then I sent him to Jordanian, a private school, the same school as King Hussein. They speak English there. My son is studying to be a biochemist. My daughter has her Master's degree. I worked at the UN for 18 years and I was an accountant. I'm retired. I'm driving to make money to help get my kids through school without saddling them with a huge debt. I don't like debt and paying interest. When I use my credit card, I pay everything when it is due. I don't spend more than I have." When he touched on the debt American kids are burdened with upon their graduation, my mind stayed on that subject. I've always felt it was a disgrace that this rich nation can't find a better way to educate its children than by forcing them to mortgage their future.

Obviously, my Jordanian friend was proud of his children. I resisted the temptation to play the "can-you-top-this" game or "upmanship" game and tell him about my children. I did, however, rehearse in my mind my children's accomplishments. Our son, Herb Jr., the baby, whom his siblings call the "Prince," graduated from the University of Chicago and Georgetown Law School. Then he decided to switch to education, and is now a Principal at a Middle School in Brooklyn. Our youngest daughter, Dawn, is a Syracuse University graduate, an Assistant Principal, a fifth-generation preacher and a pastor of a church she founded in New Jersey. Our next daughter, Sharon, going up the scale, is in the real estate business, is a professional performer, organized a Talent Tot Enterprise—teaching movement, music and dance to children. She is the National Director of the Music and Arts Departments at our church, Executive Director of one of our non-profit agencies, and she is a Dartmouth College graduate. Our first-born daughter, Leah, also a Dartmouth graduate, is a pastor too. She founded and pastors a church in Washington, D.C. She is the National Administrator of our church. She is the Chief of Staff of the National Democratic Committee and is Chief Executive Officer of the National Democratic Convention. And that is where I am headed.

Rather than have the above conversation with my driver, partly because, as I stated, I don't like upmanship or "I'm-as-good-you-are"; and, importantly, because I found it exceedingly more pleasant to reflect on the Convention. This reflection, I might add, started in earnest during the night as I fell asleep and continued with the rising of the sun. I found myself reflecting on Leah's achievements, particularly her work with the Democratic Party as its Chief of Staff and as the CEO of the convention; and my interest and role once I had arrived.

My wife and I had already been given a schedule of events. There would be a special event for parents of staff. And I had been informed I would be doing the invocation at the DNC's closing meeting, the last official item on the agenda for the convention. It is where the party's Presidential and Vice-Presidential candidates meet with the party's bigwigs. Thinking only in human terms, if one were going to choose the most important event to have a prayer, this would be the place. I had done the invocation before the DNC in 1992, when Clinton and Gore were the standard bearers. They went on to win the general election.

I thought about other Conventions I had attended and my participation in them. There was the San Francisco Convention in 1984. It was the Convention where Jesse Jackson played an important role. It was the most significant Presidential run by an African American up to that time. [I had been with Jesse from the beginning. It was in September of 1983 that we convened at my church in New York to discuss whether he should run. All across the country there had been a resounding, "Run Jesse Run." When he addressed the assemblage, he said, "I don't want 'run Jesse run' to become 'see Jessie run.' So there are three things I need if I'm going to run; machinery, masses and money."] At that convention, I was floor manager. Alexis Herman, who later became the CEO of the 1992 Convention in New York, and later became U.S. Secretary of Labor, was also there.

Jesse ran again in 1988. I didn't bother to attend that convention for reasons I don't care to discuss. The 1992 convention was in New York. As already stated, I did the invocation at the DNC's Convention meeting. I did not attend another Convention until 2004 in Boston, where I served on the Credentials Committee.

So now, here we are in 2008 at another convention. This time, however, it is super special. An African American will become the Democratic Presidential nominee, for the first time. And he has a good chance of becoming the next President of the United States. And an African American woman, who happens to be our daughter, stands in charge of the Democratic Convention. It is the stuff of which dreams are made.

Arrival in Denver

WE LANDED AT THE DENVER AIRPORT AT 2:46 PM (MOUNTAIN Time). I was met at baggage claim by two Democratic National Convention Committee ("DNCC") volunteers: a portly African American woman, maybe in her sixties, named Sandy, and a young woman, maybe in her late teens or early twenties, slender, eye-glass-wearing Euro-ethnic, named Sophia. What a contrast! I thought to myself. They were overwhelmingly friendly. They wore orange colored t-shirts with a blue square in front with the DNCC lettering.

After helping me secure my baggage and insisting on carrying it, which made me feel uncomfortable — allowing this elderly woman with this young girl to be saddled with my luggage — we went to the waiting car. On the sidewalk, like swarming bees, there were about ten volunteers. They were all super friendly. Of course, recognizing that I was Leah's dad, added a little more zest to their friendliness.

My driver, in the donated black SUV, was a wiry woman. It was hard to tell her age. She was on the smallish side. There was a weather-beaten toughness about her. (I learned later she had been a Girl Scout and her husband a Boy Scout. They loved to go camping, sleeping in tents and stuff.) Her name was Ann.

It's a 45-minute drive during rush time (30 minutes regular time) from the airport to the downtown area, more specifically, to the Teatro Hotel, where my wife and I were staying. We rode along Tuskegee Airmen Memorial Drive. I wondered who was responsible for naming the highway. I never thought of Denver as concerned about African American history. Denver, I'm told, is only 7% black.

As we started down the highway, Ann immediately commenced praising Leah. She said, "She has a done a phenomenal job. I've been involved in Democratic politics for 27 years. I've never seen any meeting as organized." I asked, "How is Denver receiving the convention?" "Oh, everybody is excited," she replied. "There were thousands of volunteers, far more volunteers than needed. The involvement is astounding. For years at the caucuses, it would be one or two persons and myself seated at the table. The last meeting, the auditorium where we hold our meetings was packed."

The Teatro Hotel is a quaint unimposing eight-story red brick building. It had been used by Colorado University. Then it was made into a hotel. It sits in the theater district on the corner of 14th Street and Arapahoe. Around it, construction was in full swing. In fact, all across downtown Denver and beyond, huge cranes could be seen. The construction significantly blocked the view from certain rooms in the hotel. The room was small but very comfortable. A beige eggshell-white décor gave it a relaxing feeling. We only stayed in this room for a day. Tomorrow, we were told, we would be moving to the presidential suite on the 8th floor which gave us a semi-unimpeded view of the mountains and the downtown area.

As I settled in the room, my wife gave me the hotel publication, named "The Play Bill," volume 4 issue 8 August 2008. She had already informed me that the Play Bill, placed in every room of the hotel, featured a glowing tribute to Leah, complete with a picture. The reader, I'm sure, will forgive a proud father's desire to share an excerpt of the article:

> This month we are taking a small step away from the Stage Door to highlight a very important person to Hotel Teatro and, on a far greater scale, to the City of Denver. Reverend Leah Daughtry was a regular visitor for months as she started preparations for the Democratic National Convention as CEO of the Democratic National Convention Committee. Leah Daughtry was a lovely guest. Now in residence in Denver, we still enjoy her kind words and gregarious nature when she stops by.
>
> Her placid demeanor and sense of humor belie the staggering responsibilities that Leah Daughtry was invited by DNC Chairman Howard Dean to take on in preparation for the 2008 Democratic National Convention. As CEO of the DNC Committee, Rev. Daughtry's vision has been enlightened and fresh, enriched by her years of public service.
>
> A humble person, she commented on her designation. "I am honored to be a part of this exciting endeavor… to elect the next Democratic President of the United States…"
>
> When the dust settles, we will all be the better for

having been acquainted with this fabulous woman. Rev. Daughtry, you are always welcome at Hotel Teatro. We'll hope to see you soon!

My daughter Sharon, with other members of the family, including my wife, daughter Dawn and her husband Todd, our son Dan with his wife Danielle had already arrived in Denver. (I was the last family member to arrive.) At 4:30 pm I received a call to meet at the Pepsi Center at 5:45 pm. My wife and I arrived at 5:30.

Podium Preview Party

ON FRIDAY EVENING, MY WIFE, KAREN, AND I WENT TO THE PEPSI Center to attend Governor Dean's Podium Preview Party. The events of the evening entailed a reception for the party delegates and workers; reviewing of the Pepsi Center and picture taking with Leah and Governor Howard Dean, Chair of the Democratic National Committee (DNC).

Upon our arrival, we were escorted to the Elite Lounge, where other party guests were mingling. We were greeted with the usual gushy friendliness and lavish compliments for Leah. The room was situated off to the left as you enter the arena; there was nothing fancy about it. The reception room was dimly lit off to the left. The dimness was enhanced by the black seats. Hors d'oeuvres including fruit and vegetable platters with the dips, cheese and crackers, shrimp cocktail, and light beverages were served by circulating waiters and waitresses. Also there was the hot food on burners which I did not open, because I knew it would be animal flesh.

The first person we met was Ms. Elbra Wedgeworth, a sizeable, affable woman. She was coordinator of the host committee. With her was an intern named Terrence. He works in Mayor Corey Booker's office in Newark, NJ.

When Leah arrived, with her sisters, brother, and in-laws in tow, she immediately rushed to me and gave me a big hug, and then her mother. After chatting for a bit, she moved swiftly to greet the other guests, a mix of Democratic Party officials, Denver elected officials, donors, supporters, and other VIPs. I marveled at the little baby I once brought home in the crook of my arm now moving confidently, comfortably and enthusiastically among the VIPs. She, who had been so withdrawn, unassuming, but always thoughtful, considerate, organized, systematic and in charge, was now publicly outgoing, gregarious and seemingly loving every minute. She seemed much more relaxed and really happier than when I saw her last, which was in June when she came to preach at my 50th Pastoral Anniversary and was in the throes of finalizing many of the hairy details of convention planning.

[Also, in July, the *New York Times* published an article highly critical of Leah and the DNCC for their handling of the convention. The article accused Leah of being behind schedule in contractual arrangements, over budget, and engaging in extravagant and unnecessary spending. Leah and Party Chairman Howard Dean responded that, in fact, all contracts had been executed on schedule, and spending was below the budget. The article had confused (it is questionable whether or not it was deliberate) the responsibilities of the Denver Host Committee and the DNCC. It was the Host Committee that had missed its fund-raising deadlines, and that had planned various receptions with questionable menus.]

Denver's mayor, John Hickenlooper, with white, open collar shirt, came to greet us. He is a restaurateur by profession, and is widely credited with popularizing the concept of micro-beer brewing. He was ebullient, perpetually smiling, and obviously very happy. Over the two years of convention planning he and Leah had become great friends.

Soon, Leah called the room to attention and made brief remarks, thanking everybody for their support during the convention planning period. She then informed us that we would now be going to have a first look at the transformed arena, now Convention Hall, and we would have the opportunity to take pictures on the podium with Governor Dean.

The arena, normally the home court of the Denver Nuggets basketball team, had undergone a dramatic change since we were here in February 2008. On the floor level CNN, FOX, and NBC networks had mini-broadcast studios. Up among the skyboxes they had larger studios, and other networks were present there as well. The ceiling of the arena was a mass of wiring and steel fixtures running across, crisscrossing and hanging down. There was a blue color motif. A thick blue rug covered the floor. The stage area was predominantly blue with, of course, some red and white. There were flashing lights and stars. It was a thing of awesome beauty.

After we completed the picture-taking session, Leah took us, the family, on a guided tour throughout the arena. She started with where she would be seated during the proceedings—the first chair on the left side of the podium – and where the Party Chair, Convention Chair, and other democratic leadership would sit.

She took us to the pathway that led to the entrance to the podium. The place where the speakers stand before taking the podium is called "The Alamo." It is the "last stand" before the speakers go forth to face the audience. Then we were taken up to the skyboxes where VIPs would gather. We were shown the offices, reception rooms, dining and drinking areas.

Standing in front of the skyboxes reserved for the CEO, we had a panoramic view across the empty arena. Leah informed us where each state delegation would be seated and why they would be seated in the assigned place. The whole thing, as in everything else in these conventions, is predominantly political. For example, the nominee's home state is traditionally assigned the best seats in the house: directly in front of the podium. Other states, such as the Party Chairman's home state, are also given priority.

Leah enlightened us as to how delegates' votes would be counted. They would use the latest high tech computers. "Are the computers purchased?" a question was asked "They're either loaned or donated," Leah answered. "What happens to them after the convention?" "The donated computers are given to the schools or other non-profits." said Leah. "What about New York public schools?" persisted another questioner "Nope, local schools or non-profits are the only recipients.

Another interesting place she showed us was the Speech Rehearsal Room, where the speakers practiced their speeches before going on stage. There are Teleprompters and televisions in which the speakers can see or hear themselves. There is a speech coach who sits nearby to observe the exercise. By the time the speaker actually goes to the podium to speak live, he or she has practiced his or her speech numerous times, and has been monitored and coached vigilantly to prevent any mistakes.

After our tour, we returned to the hotel as we had arrived, in a SUV supplied by the hotel. Tomorrow we would have our own car. As I made ready for bed, I kept thinking what a day it had been. It was now 10:30 pm Mountain Time, which made it 12:30 am Eastern Daylight Time. I had started the day in New Jersey at 4:30 am (my usual rising time); I had traveled in two cars, two planes, been in four cities and been on the move for 20 hours. I was delightfully, gratefully, slightly weary but I was too excited to be tired.

· · ·

SATURDAY, AUGUST 23, 2008
Joe Biden Named as Obama's Vice President

I RETURNED FROM WHAT SOME CALL, AND I USED TO CALL, EXercise, at 7:20 am. I had started at 6:10 am. I had been up since 2:20 am. Sometime ago, when I realized that I was doing more than physical exercise, I started calling it the exercise "The Total Worship Experience." This is because during the time of my physical exercise, which included walking, running and sometimes shadowboxing, I would do mental exercises, including concentration, memorization, prayer, meditation and breathing exercises. When all parts of our being are concentrated on communion with God, it is total worship. So, I've come to call my morning ritual "TWE" or "Total Worship Experience."

It was revealed to me a long time ago that physical care of our bodies was a form of worship. This physical care is a way of honoring God who gave us our bodies, which house our spirits. The Bible says, "Know ye not your bodies are the temple of the Holy Spirit which dwelleth in you which you have from God? And that you are not your own…?" When a tenant takes care of his or her rented house, he/she is respecting the landlord who rented it to him/her.

When I returned to my room, my wife met me with the news, "So, Obama picked Biden." "Oh yeah? Is that right?" I asked. " Haven't you heard?" she asked. "No I've been away from the news sources. But I'm not surprised. I have been telling people I thought it would be Biden," I answered. I thought that Biden brought qualities and experiences that would compliment Obama.

- Biden has known McCain for 30 years. He knows McCain's weaknesses and strengths.

- He has a "working class, blue collar, lunch bucket" background. He was born in Scranton, PA. Pennsylvania is an important swing state. It, like Ohio, is made up of the class and color of people that Obama lost overwhelmingly to Clinton.
- Also, in that same vein, Biden has been a staunch supporter of police and firemen.
- He is a Roman Catholic, another large population with which Obama has had problems.
- Biden is indisputably a foreign policy expert. McCain has consistently hammered Obama on his inexperience in foreign policy.
- Biden has experience in many areas. He was chair of the Judiciary Committee. He has worked well with the opposition. He is well liked across the board in Congress and the media.
- Biden's age leaves him outside of the possibility of a run for the Presidency should Obama lose. When a selected Vice President is young and has ambition, they can sometimes get distracted.
- Biden is not a rich man.
- Biden cannot be considered an absolute insider. While he has been in the Senate for over 30 years, he goes home to Delaware every evening. He made a promise standing at the bedside of his son, who had been injured in a car accident that had killed both his wife and daughter, that he would come home every evening after he completed his day of work in the Senate. So every evening, he takes the long train ride from Washington to Delaware.

- Biden is a friend to the Clintons. This should help with the unity challenge.
- Biden also has a good relationship with the women's community, having supported legislation that is favorable to women. I believe that this should help win over women who are supporters of Senator Clinton.
- Biden has "fire in his belly." He is very passionate about what he believes.
- He is a good speaker and an excellent debater.
- Biden is known to be tough. There is a story of a young Biden running into his childhood home, crying because someone in the neighborhood had been beaten him up. His mother told him to go back out into the streets and bloody the nose of whomever it was that attacked him. In addition, it worth noting in his early years he was a stutterer. Through sheer determination, he became quite proficient in the use of language.

But, on the negative side, there are some things that Obama has to be concerned about.

- There are the campaign attacks which Biden launched against Obama. McCain will surely use these attacks. In fact, almost as soon as the Biden Vice Presidential announcement was made, McCain ran a television ad showing Biden questioning Obama's experience, saying Obama wasn't ready to be President.
- Biden's garrulity. He loves to talk and in general, anyone who talks too much makes mistakes.
- He is prone to gaffe.

However, when Biden's positives are placed beside the negatives, it is obvious that the positives far outweigh the negatives.

Personally, I like Biden. I don't know him but those who do tend to say nice things about him. I like his stand on Darfur. He advocated using force there if necessary.

The only item on today's agenda was a meeting Leah was having with the Brooklyn volunteers. The meeting was held in her suite at the Hyatt Regency. The suite was expansive and palatial. There was a kitchen, dining area, huge living room, which was connected to a conference room, and a large bedroom with its own sitting area, bathroom and dressing room. It was on the 38th floor with a full view of the majestic, imposing Rocky Mountains. It was a luxurious setting that must've required one to have extraordinary determination to leave it to go face the challenges of the world.

After introductions, and unanimous expressions of gratitude for the opportunity to participate in "this historic event," the meeting covered:

- Leah's schedule of events to be shared only with the family members.
- A general schedule of events.
    - Qualifications and dissemination of credentials. Unlike the Republican Convention, new, different credentials would be issued each day. Considerable discussion was given to who would receive them and from where they would be distributed. There was a room specifically set aside for the guests of Chairman Dean and the CEO, Leah, to pick their credentials up.
- Host responsibilities in key areas i.e. guest and VIP lounges, skyboxes and VIP offices.
- Managing reception areas. Making sure that food and drinks were sufficiently provided.

The meeting started at 2:15 pm and lasted 50 minutes, until 3:05 pm. Everybody was excited. The appreciation was obvious. In addition to the official photographer, it seemed that everybody had a camera.

Credentials and Skyboxes

LEAH WAS HER USUAL CALM, RELAXED, CONFIDENT SELF. SHE was clearly in command and had an extra touch of humor. She explained each category and assignment in detail and patiently answered all questions. One of her advance men, a member of our church in Brooklyn, whispered to me, referencing an earlier meeting they had attended, "Leah was special at that meeting." As he shook his head in amazement, he kept repeating "Little Leah." He was making reference to Leah's early childhood. He had watched her grow up in the church. "She is something special," he whispered with a broad smile on his face.

Family members had special responsibilities. Sharon, early on, was given the assignment of authorizing, sorting and distributing credentials. At the Convention, she commanded Leah's credentials operation day and night. It was, as one can imagine, a tension-packed, beehive of activity. Everyone wanted credentials. And they were not satisfied with just credentials. They wanted special credentials!

There were a variety of credentials available. Each gave a different level of access, had a different color and had to be picked up anew every day for that day's activities in the Pepsi Center. The categories and colors of the credentials (from least to greatest access) were:

ARENA (orange)
SPECIAL GUEST (lavender)
HONORED GUEST (purple)
FLOOR (green)

BACKSTAGE (blue)
PODIUM (red)

Arena credentials provided the least amount of access and mobility in and around the Pepsi Center. Podium allowed the greatest mobility with access to all areas of the Pepsi center including backstage and the actual podium from which the speakers delivered their speeches. And the ones in between allowed graduated levels of access. There were also individual passes that provided access to lounges and skyboxes.

Needless to say, everybody wanted the credentials that would allow as much access and mobility as possible, especially to the coveted seats in the skyboxes. But because of the limited amount of space in the boxes, the owner of the box could only give passes to a select and limited group of people. Obviously, the Chairman and the CEO had their own skyboxes. And Obama's special people and other VIPs also had their own skyboxes. The owners of these skyboxes were perpetually bombarded with requests for access. This was, in part, because depending on where the box was located, the view to the entire convention floor and stage was impeccable. Another factor was the mélange of persons in the box. Anyone, from company CEOs, to stars of television, movies and stage, to high-ranking politicos, to ambassadors to and from countries, to heads of major church denominations, could be found in the boxes. These boxes were a veritable "Who's Who in America." Equally as important was the fact that these boxes were stocked with beverages of every description, food, snacks and cushioned seats.

Leah had two boxes. Box 18 was on the first level, which was called the Club level, and Box 69 was on the second level. Box 69 had a special seating section attached below it that contained 40 seats. Then in the actual box, where the food and drinks were, there were 12 seats plus a counter and

6 stools and a bit of standing room. In total, 25 persons total could fit inside the box at a time. Because of the huge amount of requests for access, each night different guests were invited and rotated in and out of the box.

To repeat, it was Sharon's responsibility to manage Leah's credentials. While her role was obscure, the importance of the task was crucial. A mix up with the credentials could create a riot. Sharon, doing her job so well, contributed to the success of the convention. Dawn's responsibility was to be Leah's assistant, accompanying her wherever she went, catering to her every need. Dawn's husband, Todd, was one of Leah's advance persons. My daughter-in-law, Danielle, managed Skybox 18, and my, niece, Deborah, along with Sharon and Dawn, managed Skybox 69. Chyann, one of the very efficient and dependable teenage members from our church in Brooklyn, along with my grandson, Lorenzo, and my two nephews, Marcus and Andrew, were pages to the Chairman. A page is responsible for shadowing the person to whom they are assigned as well as for completing tasks given to them by this person. The page program, which was managed by Jacqueline Williams of our church in Washington, DC, provided extraordinary experience, contact and access for our teenagers.

The Convention's housing director was Tina Akintayo. She is a childhood friend of Leah's and, like Leah, grew up in our church. Her family members are some of the strongest in our church. Tina had a staggering responsibility: arranging rooms for over 20,000 people. And it seemed that everybody demanded the best rooms, changed their plans at the last minute and demanded to be accommodated even when the deadline to book a room had passed weeks before. Everybody suddenly became a VIP and wanted suites. But somehow, with God's help and the help of Leah and the rest of her staff, Tina managed to be completely successful.

After the meeting, I returned to my room and spent the rest of the day reflecting on the day's events. I pondered the rest of the Convention, trying to absorb it all, while watching the political pundits offering their analyses.

SUNDAY, AUGUST 24
The Interfaith Gathering

AT 6 AM, I WAS IN THE STREETS FOR MY YOTAL WORSHIP EXperience. It was a clear lovely morning. The mountains, with white clouds surrounding the top, were majestic. I was overwhelmed with gratitude. I could not stop the fountains within from pouring forth gratitude and praise.

Upon returning to the hotel, I did a radio interview with the *New York Post*. The interviewer wanted to know what impact Obama was making on the black community. My response was, "Obama is making an impact not only on the black community, but also on the world. There will be people all across the globe, especially young people and so-called minority men and women, black and white, who will draw inspiration from his achievements."

Afterwards, as my wife and I sat at breakfast, Leah called. "Why aren't you at the parent's breakfast?" she asked. The breakfast was scheduled to begin 9:50 am and it was now 10 am. We packaged our breakfast, dressed, and hastened to the 38th floor of the Grand Hyatt. There we found a panoramic view of the city and the mountains in the distance. There were about 75 DNCC staffers and their parents in the room. After making laudatory comments about my wife and me, Leah had departed for her next engagement.

We were immediately inundated with congratulations and praise for Leah. The most memorable commendation was made by Mr. Tom Brooks of AT&T, who sponsored the program. He said, "I have attended many conventions but this is the best organized. Leah is phenomenal. Not only is she efficient, but she has such a cordial and pleasant spirit. Her staff does too. In fact, I'm sure that they are a reflection of her spirit. It has been a joy working with her."

It was difficult leaving this high place with this breathtaking view. But after greetings, handshakes, and a few hugs, we reluctantly bade farewell to the smiling hosts. We received our gift bags, entered our waiting car, and headed back to the hotel. Each gift bag, given to each parent, contained the uniquely special gift of a 4x4 tag featuring a picture of their offspring. This tag was attached to a string which could be placed around the neck. On our tags were the words "I belong to Leah."

The next event was the Interfaith Gathering, scheduled to begin at 2 pm. We arrived at 1 pm and were taken to the holding room. Every major event had a holding room for VIPs and/or speakers who need time to gather themselves or to relax in order to prepare for the schedule event.

Bishop Charles Blake Sr., a tall, cordial man, with a solemn aura, is the Presiding Prelate of the 12,000 congregations of the Churches of God in Christ (COGIC) International. He was already present, as were his assistants. One in particular, Reverend Eugene Rivers, had previously been a minister in our church. He's a rather interesting young man. He went straight from the streets of Philadelphia to the classrooms of Harvard University. After earning straight A's, the administration discovered that he never matriculated!

Entering the room, brash and garrulous, was Sister Helen Prejean, activist, author, and Roman Catholic nun. She is well known for having written the bestselling book, made into a movie, *Dead Man Walking*. She is also a chaplain. A short, plucky woman, she was dressed in a gray chalk-striped suit. Immediately she asked Leah, "How did I get here?" Leah explained, "I invited you. You were my first choice. I got all my first choices." Assemblywoman Annette M. Robinson of Brooklyn and Reverend Cheryl Anthony came into the room. Annette and I shared memories of Leah growing up. Both of our eyes watered with tears.

When all of the participants assembled, they marched out into the 4,000-seat auditorium to a standing ovation. It was 2 pm. Prior to the procession, there was a musical prelude, which focused primarily upon Negro spirituals, sung by the Spirituals Project of Denver, Colorado. The Denver Indian Singers, a Native American drumming and singing ensemble, led the processional. The ceremony was opened with prayer and litany offered by Reverend Lucia Guzman, Imam Mohammad Mardini, Rabbi Amy Schwartzman, and Dr. Patrick Whelan.

After this, Leah did the welcome and statement of purpose. Her statement lasted approximately 5minutes. In the statement, she recounted the history of the ecumenical gathering and what the Faith in Action Committee hoped to accomplish. Greetings were then offered by Colorado Governor Bill Ritter, followed by a musical selection by Richard Smallwood & Vision. It was a rousing, house-rocking musical rendition. Next, readings from the Torah, the Sutra Nipata, the Holy Qur'an and the Holy Bible were rendered.

There were four major speakers, each of whom addressed topics related to the human family. These topics all fell under the heading of "Our Sacred Responsibility." The topics, along with the presenters, were as follows:

- Our Sacred Responsibility to Our Children, Bishop Charles E. Blake
- Our Sacred Responsibility to Our Neighbor, Rabbi Dr. Tzvi Hersh Weinreb
- Our Sacred Responsibility to Our Nation, Sister Helen Prejean

- Our Sacred Responsibility to Our World, Dr. Ingrid Mattson

The closing prayer and litany were read by Imam Abdur-Rahim Ali, Dr. Polly Baca, Reverend Dr. Shaun Casey and Rabbi Marc Schneier. The Trinity United Methodist Choir of Denver provided recessional music.

It was an impressive ceremony. The audience was completely enthralled and involved. There were the Pentecostals, who did not hesitate to give expression to their emotions and sentiments. And there was also the deep reflective silence of the other religious participants. However, and unfortunately, before the ceremony started, there were loud demonstrators. Several pro-life protestors, holding up placards and chanting pro-life slogans, were hastily escorted from the auditorium. There was no violence.

All of the participants were excellent, persuasive, bold and eloquent. They spoke to their particular issues, which they were free to do. Bishop Blake said he was a pro-life democrat and felt that someone had to speak up for babies in the womb. But he was equally harsh in his criticism of those who fight for the unborn in the body and do nothing for babies outside of the body. He concluded his speech with a reference to the Olympics. He recalled that in two of the track races, runners were disqualified because they dropped the baton. He challenged, "We must not drop the baton. We must pass it on." Sister Helen Prejean assailed the death penalty. She called it murder. She said the violence against those who are sentenced to death, is also mental violence against them. The anguish that those on death row suffer is unbearable. Her presentation exceeded all others in applause. The Muslim woman expressed her love and support for America. Muslims are a part of the United States of America and are even represented in the military. But she was strongly critical of the stereotyping of Muslims.

The theme of the ceremony might have been *love*. Practically all the speakers cited variations of the love theme from their holy book and tradition. Rabbi Dr. Tzvi Hersh Weinreb said, "Love your neighbor as yourself." He then asked "Who is my neighbor?" He proceeded to answer by citing all the classes, colors, and religions represented in the human family.

This ecumenical gathering was historic. It was the first time the Democrats held a religious/spiritual ceremony as a part of their convention. It was also a climax to four years of work promoting public expression of commitment to religious values.

It is Leah who organized the Faith in Action Committee. Her team succeeded in showing America that Republicans do not have a monopoly on God and religion. She has been given credit for inspiring Democratic leaders to express themselves publicly regarding their religious faith, and also for the significant increase in the percentage of religious people participating in the Democratic Party.

The last public event for the day was the delegates' party in support for the Katrina victims. It, too, was held in the Colorado Civic Center. It was crowded and noisy as thousands packed the center. Inside, the music blasted away and could even be heard outside in the hallway. There was free food and drinks across the entire auditorium.

After hearing Chairman Dean and Leah address the gathering, I walked back to the hotel, only four blocks from the Center. It had been a long eventful day. I wanted time to savor all that had happened.

One of the tension points that never became public was the insistence of atheists to participate in the interfaith service. I wish I could tell you the logic of atheists demanding to participate in a religious ceremony with believers. Nevertheless, there was a demand for equal participation and recognition. In the end, Leah decided against their participation and atheists were not on the program. There was another challenge from those who resisted the idea of religion mixing with politics. Surely, they had a far more persuasive argument than the above-mentioned atheists. Nonetheless, Leah was also able to resolve this challenge.

I concluded the day with a one-hour radio interview with Reverend Conrad Tilliard, who was sitting in for Gary Imhotep Bird. We concentrated primarily on issues surrounding Crown Heights, Brooklyn, New York. This was the 17th year anniversary of the killing of Gavin Cato and the violent reaction from the community that followed. So, I had started and ended the day on the radio.

MONDAY, AUGUST 25
African American Caucus Meeting

AFTER A SHORT TOTAL WORSHIP EXPERIENCE FROM 6:10 AM TO 7 am, I spent the rest of the morning on the telephone and catching up on my journal entries.

The first event of the day was the African American Caucus meeting, comprised of all African American delegates as well as other interested observers. The convention schedule allows for the various caucuses (i.e., African American, Hispanic, Asian and now the Faith Caucus) to have their own meeting time. For example, the African American Caucus met on Monday and Wednesday from 10 am–12 pm in the Wells Fargo Room of the Colorado Civic Center (CCC), which is a mammoth construction, covering two square blocks. All of the Caucus meetings were held at the CCC.

Mike, my faithful driver, was waiting to drive me the short distance from the hotel to the CCC. I could've walked, but I was late and Mike seemed to enjoy doing his job. Mike is in his 50s or 60s. He is Caucasian, with an oval face, receding hairline and small eyes covered with eyeglasses.

By now, the crowd had increased considerably inside and outside of the center. An assortment of people was clustered on the sidewalk in front of the center. The number of protestors had multiplied. There were the ever-present pro-lifers, holding up placards with a picture of a bloody, deformed fetus with a grainy picture of a Barack Obama on the side. Another group held up McCain signs while shouting his praises. Still another group, a religious sect named Fulan Gong, showed pictures of bodies murdered and tortured, supposedly by the Chinese government. Some of the Fulan Gong distributed leaflets, while others sat in a trance-like state. Some time ago, I participated in a rally in Union Square in New York with them. They charged China with numerous human rights violations. Of course, our interest in participating was to protest China's support for the government of Sudan.

I did not have my credentials but I didn't want to wait on the long line to pick them up. So I called Leah's Chief of Operations, Lisa, an efficient, pleasant young lady. She brought my credentials to me, and then drove me to the meeting in a golf cart. Riding through the Center gave me an appreciation of how huge the place was. We wove in and out of the moving crowds. Everybody had their credentials around their necks and seemed intent on getting to somewhere important.

The Wells Fargo auditorium was about half full when I finally arrived, and I was just in time to hear Leah being introduced. When she came forward to speak, she spoke of her years as a Civil Rights baby. She was born August 27, 1963, the day before the March on Washington. She mentioned my dilemma: going to Washington or staying home with my wife and new baby. I had decided to stay home. She concluded her remarks with a conversation she had had with Congressman John Lewis, former chair of the Student Non-Violent Coordinating Committee (SNCC). He was one of the demonstrators beaten on the Edmund Pettus Bridge in Selma, Alabama. The intention of the demonstrators was to walk the 50-mile highway to Montgomery, Alabama. She said that Mr. Lewis had told her that when he was preparing to leave home to join Dr. King in the Movement, his father had given him one piece of advice: "When you go, *get in the way.*" Leah's challenge to the audience was to "*Get in the way*—don't sit on the sidelines. Don't be idle, but get involved, make a difference!"

She received a standing ovation. Listening and leaning against the wall as she spoke were Geoffrey Canada, a great organizer, administrator, humanitarian and CEO of Children's Zone in Harlem, NY, and Marc Morial, President of the National Urban League. They were ready to go onto the stage for a panel discussion. They each gave enthusiastic greetings, and were congratulatory of Leah's accomplishments.

When Leah finally finished, she descended the stairs to a waiting crowd that had gathered around the stage. They extended hands to shake. There were hugs and papers, cards and books to autograph. Cameras were clicking. Everybody was making requests. People came to me to arrange photo sessions.

I fleetingly remembered the experience I had when it became known I was Tupac Shakur's pastor. Youngsters would descend on me for autographs. As I made ready to sign my name they would say, "Put down that you are Tupac's pastor."

As I followed Leah toward the vestibule, people were stopping her all along the way. People were taking pictures, shaking hands, extending congratulations and always expressing how proud of her they were. I thought to myself, I have been in the middle many of these encircling crowds full of wide-eyed smiling people. And I, myself, have been the recipient of these heaping shows of adulation on numerous occasions. But I never thought I would be following one of my children almost completely unnoticed. Occasionally an old friend recognized me. I felt no jealousy or desire to get in the middle of it. Instead I was filled with gratitude and admiration, grateful for what my daughter had accomplished. I had such profound gratitude for having lived to see our prayers and parental guidance produce such outstanding results.

An old friend, Texas State Senator Al Edwards, joined the moving crowd around Leah. Again, we shared our memories of Leah growing up. Al remembered her from the early years of the Black United Front. When we arrived in the corridor, we met CNN analyst Donna Brazile. I remembered when Donna cut her political teeth as a youth organizer in the Jackson campaign of 1984. Yvette Clark, Congresswoman from the 11th Congressional district in Brooklyn was also there. I watched Yvette grow up in Brooklyn. She was one of the early recipients of the Randolph Evans Memorial Scholarship Fund, which we had created in 1979 in memory of 15-year-old Randy Evans, who was killed by a New York City policeman in 1976 for no reason at all. (In 1977, the jury pretty much acquitted the killer cop. We organized the fury of the community in a boycott. Our organizing efforts eventuated into the New York Metropolitan Black United Front and later into the National Black United Front. Every year, since 1979, we have given ten college-bound students a scholarship of $1500 in the name of Randy Evans.) Councilwoman Darlene Mealy **of** the 41st District in Brooklyn was there; I remembered when she won the seat in an upset of the Boyland family's candidate.

All of these women are competent, committed, concerned and always cordial. In addition, Reverend Joseph Lowery, veteran Civil Rights activist, was there. It was sad to see him in a wheelchair, but his voice was still strong and, as always, critical of something. In this case, he had not received the accommodations that he sought. I told him I would try to fix it.

Convention Opening Session

I WALKED BACK TO THE HOTEL. SO MUCH WAS ON MY MIND and I still had obligations to take care of back home. By the time I settled into my room, word came to me: we should leave early for the opening session of the Convention. Immediately, I summoned my driver and made ready to depart. The streets to the Pepsi Center were packed. Ordinarily, it should have taken 10 to 15 minutes to drive to the Pepsi Center; today it would take 30 minutes. The opening session was scheduled to commence at 3 pm. We arrived at 2:15 pm. Law-enforcement officers were ubiquitous. Getting into the center was a slow process. The security was slow and thorough. There were three security stops that must have had every available electronic device ever created. At the last stop, we disembarked from the car. The hood, the trunk, and underneath the vehicles were scrutinized. Dogs brought their sniffing skills to the occasion. Our bags were checked as we walked through more security. It was a good thing that we had left the hotel at 1:45 pm. I f it took this long for those of us in the VIP entourage, it would take considerably more time for the ordinary driver. In fact, cars were parked at a great distance from the center, requiring a lengthy walk.

On our way in, I felt the excitement in the air. I have practiced staying calm for so many years that I seldom let my emotions free. But I could not help allowing some internal emotional release as we rode through the streets seeing the crowds of people, feeling the energy and knowing that our daughter would be making one of the opening speeches of the convention.

Entering the VIP section, I stopped to say hello to news commentator Roland Martin. He seemed to be engrossed in something and his mind was clearly not with me as we conversed. He wasn't friendly, but I attributed this to his preoccupation. We went on in and located our Boxes, Box 18 on the first level and Box 69 on the second level. These perfectly placed boxes were several tiers up, and looked down on the arena floor, directly in front of the podium. Everything was fine there. Snacks were plenteous. There was green salad, rolls, pasta, chips, potato salad and drinks of every description.

Then, we checked the guest lounge called Qwest Continental Divide East. This visitors' lounge had a beautiful veranda looking out into the streets. We conferred with the hostesses that had been assigned to the lounge and the boxes. Everything there was great. There was an abundance of food consisting of black bean salad, guacamole, shrimp salad, portabella mushrooms, cheese sandwiches, various cheeses and crackers, fruits, desserts and drinks. We also checked Mrs. Michelle Obama's lounge, next door at Qwest Continental Divide West.

At 3 pm, the Convention was gaveled to order and Democratic Party Chairman Howard Dean was introduced. He spoke for a few minutes, welcoming the delegates and supporters, and thanking the host committee. By the time he introduced Leah, our boxes were crowded. Dr. Adelaide Sanford, Dr. Sheila Tranum, AME Zion Bishop Dennis Proctor and other church, community and family members had joined us.

Leah stepped briskly to the podium. Her blue jacket and skirt blended ideally with the blue motif on the stage and podium. She confidently started her speech with her hands firmly on the sides of the podium. Her voice was strong, clear, and rhythmic. During her speech, she spoke of the failures of the Bush administration and reminded the crowd of their responsibility as Democrats to fight for the well-being of all—not just some—of our nation's citizens.

I stood enthralled, fighting to keep my mind in the present. I occasionally, briefly, lost the battle. My mind insisted on carrying me backward. I remembered when she was just a wee baby curled in the crook of my arms on the day I brought her home from the hospital. I remembered walking her to school and fighting with the principal to challenge her intelligence. He eventually did. She was skipped a grade. He wanted to skip her two grades but I resisted. I recalled teaching her the ABCs. I had also taught her the Greek alphabet when I was studying New Testament Greek at New York Theological Seminary. I remembered the many trips we made together, including frequent visits to the United Nations and innumerable community meetings. I remembered our travels abroad, including the Holy Land and France. (We always encouraged our children to travel abroad; while they were in college, we encouraged them to do a semester abroad, preferably to countries other than Africa. We knew that we, as parents, would take care of travels to the Motherland. We reasoned that by visiting other countries, it would increase the family's reservoir of knowledge and experience. Sharon and Herb Jr. did semesters in Spain and Italy respectively. Dawn contemplated study abroad in Scotland, but ultimately decided against the program. Interestingly enough, if she had taken the trip, she would have been on the flight crashed over Lockerbie, Scotland.)

Leah and I had walked the streets of Paris and dined in sidewalk cafes on the Champs-Élysées. We had pondered old volumes in the library and studied historic relics in the Louvre after visiting the top of the Eiffel Tower. After two weeks in Paris, we took the train to Blois, a quaint, quiet village located 50 miles from Paris. There, Leah would study the French language, history, and culture, in a rural, person-to-person setting. I was teary-eyed when I left her there, standing on the quay in Blois.

I struggled back to the present, helped by the applause and shouts of approval from the crowd, as she made significant points in her speech. We, in the skybox could be heard shouting across the arena as she spoke. When she was finished, there was a standing ovation and loud verbal responses across the arena. In our boxes, we were all on our feet.

After she had completed her speech, my wife and I went down to her office. She was seated, quietly picking at a plate of food. We all hugged each other and were profuse in our praise. She decided to go upstairs to the boxes to greet her guests and the well-wishers. As we put our arms around each other, I prayed a brief prayer of thanksgiving and praise. On our way up to the boxes, people along the corridors were waving, smiling, and stepping forward to shake hands. When we arrived at the box, she was, once again, overwhelmed with praises, screams, hugs and kisses. It really gave me great joy to see how people across the nation responded to her. Everybody expressed love and appreciation for her, and pride over her achievements. My friends, from the most radical, revolutionary, nationalists to the most moderate and conservative and in all between, were all unanimous in their praise and appreciation. It was as if everybody had adopted Leah as his/her own daughter.

When the uproar quieted down, my wife, said, "We made the right decision." Months before the convention started, Leah had to make a decision as to whether she preferred to gavel the convention open and make brief remarks or whether she preferred to make a five-minute speech. She chose the five-minute speech. I still had doubts. Although she had a longer time to speak, she had given up the symbolism and history of opening up the convention by bringing the gavel down. What an exorbitant trade-off!

There are three other highly charged moments in the proceedings that evening: Jesse Jackson Jr.: While he was speaking, I remembered when he was just a young fellow trying to be a surrogate for his father during the 1984 Jackson candidacy for the President. I also remembered our trip abroad to Italy. Reverend Jesse Jackson had asked me to accompany him and his family on this historic trip. We met with the Pope, the Prime Minister and the U.S. Ambassador. From there, we had gone on to London, where we met with the Archbishop of Canterbury and a host of other dignitaries. During his speech, I also thought about the other children of movers and shakers who were present at the convention; Governor David Paterson, son of former New York Secretary of State, Basil Paterson; Congresswoman Yvette Clarke, daughter of former NYC Councilwoman Una Clarke; Comptroller Willie Thompson, son of Judge Willie Thompson; Assemblyman Darryl Towns, son of Congressman Ed Towns; Keith Wright, son of deceased Judge Bruce Wright; Councilwoman Diane Foster, daughter of Former Councilman Reverend Wendell Foster.

Then there was the Kennedy family: Caroline, the daughter of President John F. Kennedy, came forward and introduced her uncle, Senator Ted Kennedy. It had been rumored that he would attend the convention. When he was introduced and came on to the stage, he electrified the crowd. They stood applauding, yelling and stomping for a long time. The more he sought to quiet them, the more vigorously they applauded. So many memories flooded my mind as my eyes took in his protruding belly, round face, bent shoulders, and silver hair. I remembered when he first won the Senate seat in Massachusetts. His youthful, boyish face and energetic movements played vividly across the screen of my mind. There were memories of John's and Bobby's assassinations. There were memories, too, of Dr. King's assassination and the events and leaders of the Civil Rights Movement. He spoke briefly but gave assurance that he would be present for the inauguration of Barack Obama. I should mention that a collage of visual images on a video presentation preceded his presence. Michelle Obama and children: Another memorable moment occurred when Michelle Obama, wife of the candidate, with her children and with the television presence of Obama interacting with family, won the hearts of all. She was eloquent and winsome in her presentation. But when the surprise guest, Obama himself, played across the screen and started interacting with the children it overwhelmed the audience. There were tears of joy, applause, and nods of approval.

I returned to my hotel in a dream-like state. It was so unreal. And yet, there was the physical presence of people, which gave me the assurance that it was all very real.

TUESDAY, AUGUST 26
Hillary Clinton's Speech

IT WAS A LEISURELY MORNING, EXCEPT FOR THE WALK TO THE CCC (Colorado Convention Center). I missed my Total Worship Experience (TWE). I needed to catch up on my writing, telephone calls, and other office business. And, I wanted time to reflect on the events of the convention thus far, especially last night at Leah's speech.

Around 10 am, I went to room 101 in the Center to pick up my credentials. Guests of the Chairman and the CEO went to this special room, which had an attached lounge and food area, to get their credentials. Other people went to the Credentials Distribution Center. When I arrived, people were gathered around the tables. Credentials were distributed efficiently and with dispatch. I was proud of my daughter, Sharon, as she managed the operation and calmly responded to the many problems. She had to identify legitimate requests and deal with constant demands. Everyone was now a friend of the CEO and/or the Chairman, or the friend of the friend of the friend of the Chairman and/or the CEO. The office hours were from 8:30 am to 1 pm. Commendations must also be extended to Wilma Hubbard, Yvonne Rubie, and LaVerne Walker, all members of my church who assisted with the credentials and scheduling.

There was food, easy chairs, and television for those who wanted to lounge or relax for a while. Leah had told us that the experienced convention go-er never spends money for food. She was right. Everywhere you went, there was free food.

I tried to make it to the Faith Caucus on time. It was scheduled for 12 to 2 pm in the Korbell Room at the Center. The theme was: "Common Ground and Common Good." The subheading was, "What are the pressing moral values of the day? How can progressives and conservatives find common ground?" The attempt to bring unity to progressive and conservative religionists reminded me of similar efforts in the late '60s, during the turmoil of the Civil Rights/Black Power Movements. A colleague, Dr. Bill Bentley of Chicago, Illinois, and I had been invited to Malone College in Ohio, where liberal and conservative churchmen and women were holding a conference. They had been meeting for a long time. Our position was that while we were conservative in our theology, we were intensely progressive, even radical, in our sociopolitical ideology. This disoriented the conference participants. They seemed to have been wholly in one camp or the other. They were either conservatives or progressives. We sought to synthesize our belief system. As the debate went back and forth, I remember Dr. Hubbard, President of Fuller, the renowned conservative theological school in California, saying, "I hear my theology with which I'm in agreement. But, I don't understand the sociology with which I am not in agreement." I'm not sure if they continued to have meetings. We were never invited back.

I departed the panel discussion early. There was nothing new that encouraged me to stay and I really wanted to get ready for the night's session. Tonight would be one of the most important. What happened tonight would significantly influence the outcome of the election in November. It was Senator Hillary Clinton's night to speak.

When we arrived at the arena, we did our usual check. Everything was in order. The people were in place. You could tell as soon as you walked into the arena that there was something special about this night.

From the day that Obama gathered enough delegates to defeat Senator Clinton, there had been hard feelings. In fact, almost from the beginning of the campaign, there had been rancor and heated verbal exchanges. After Obama won his victory, with the help of a compromise in Michigan, Ohio, and Florida, many Hillary supporters were angry. Some said they would not support Obama. Others went further: they said they would support McCain.

At times, Senator Clinton, herself, seemed to be wavering in her support for Obama. Occasionally, she gave the impression that she was still trying to find a way to win. Her concession speech on the night that Obama went over the top was anything but a concession. She extolled her own achievements in the primary and sent a glimmer of hope to her supporters that victory was still possible. It was only after there seemed to be unanimous criticism from news commentators and appeals from Democratic leaders that she began to soften, at least outwardly, and accept the reality. Now the question everyone was asking with bated breath was "To what extent will she go to unite the party?"

The evening's proceedings opened at 3 pm Mountain Time, the usual starting time. As always, there were a number of speakers before the main event. Congresswoman Eleanor Holmes Norton spoke with her usual eloquence regarding the peculiar situation of Washington, D.C. They pay taxes but have no official representation in the Congress. One of the most moving speeches and sad appearances was by Ted Sorensen who was an assistant to JFK. Moving very slowly, he said he had been in search of a President that could match JFK's compassion and ability to fight for justice at home and peace around the world. He said that once in a while, history and hope meet in a man and a movement. In his lifetime he had seen this happen twice, JFK and now Obama. When he was done, slowly he hobbled behind the screen.

At 9:45 pm MT, the hour had arrived. Hillary Clinton came to the podium. She was greeted with a prolonged standing ovation, hand clapping, and foot stomping. The crowd loudly screamed her name out and it reverberated across the arena. Finally, when the crowd had settled down, she began to speak *"I am honored to be here tonight. A proud mother. A proud Democrat. A proud American. A proud supporter of Barack Obama."* There, she said it. But did she mean it? She continued *"My friends, it is time to take back the country we love, whether you voted for me or for Barack, the time is now to unite as a single party with a single purpose. We are on the same team, and none of us can sit on the sidelines. This is a fight for the future. And it's a fight we must win... No way, no how, no McCain. Barack Obama is my candidate. And he must be our President."*

Slowly, inevitably, the reality crept across the mesmerized audience. Yes! They had heard it! She continued to describe the crisis in this country, the failed policy of the Bush administration, and the similarities between Mr. Bush and Mr.

McCain. She cited the heroes and heroines of yesteryear, those who had fought for the right to vote, especially for the right of women to vote. She said, *"This is the story [referring to the people who had won the right to vote] of America. Of women and men who defy the odds and never give up. How do we give this country back to them? By following the example of a brave New Yorker, a woman who risked her life to shepherd slaves along the Underground Railroad. And on that path to freedom, Harriet Tubman had one piece of advice. 'If you hear the dogs, keep going. If you see the torches in the woods, keep going. If they're shouting after you, keep going. Don't ever stop. Keep going. If you want a taste of freedom, keep going.' Even in the darkest moments, ordinary Americans have found the faith to keep going."*

Now moving towards her conclusion, with the audience on their feet, she said *"That is our duty, to build that bright future, and to teach our children that in America there is no chasm too deep, no barrier too great, no ceiling too high for all who work hard. Never back down. Always keep going. Have faith in God, in our country and in each other."* She concluded, *"Thank you so much. God bless America."*

It was an unforgettable night and an unforgettable scene. Long, steady clapping, stomping and yelling shook the rafters of the arena. Mrs. Clinton clearly, indisputably, left no doubt that she was supporting Obama. She would be working for the unity of the Democratic Party and a better America for all. Surely, looking back at these days, historians might very well say what Winston Churchill said of England during the Second World War. This was her "finest hour."

Joining us in our box were Mrs. Jacqueline Jackson, wife of Reverend Jesse Jackson, and her children, Santita, little Jackie, Jonathan, Yusef and his wife. (I will always remember Jonathan and his thoughtfulness. As I've already mentioned, I became disappointed with Jackson's campaign of '88 and I decided not to attend the Convention in Atlanta, GA. Jonathan, who knew of my commitment to his father and the campaign, was sensitive to my feelings. In the middle of the convention, he called me just to see how I was doing and to say thank you.)

Also in the box was Mrs. Michele Paterson, wife of Governor David A. Paterson; author John Grisham who penned *A Time to Kill*, *The Pelican Brief*, and recently, *The Appeal*; Bishop Charles E. Blake, Presiding Bishop of the Churches of God in Christ, Inc. (COGIC); Congressman Bobby Scott of Virginia, in addition to other community and church people. Also, Mayor Corey Booker of Newark, NJ stopped by.

Returning to the hotel, I kept reviewing Hillary Clinton's speech and comparing it to her so-called concession speech on the night that Obama went over the top in the Democratic primary. What a difference! I was proud and glad that she had made the decision to support Obama without reservation. I was very disappointed and even angry with the way she had responded on the night he won. I have a deep admiration for the Clintons. I believed her performance that night would seriously hurt her political future, negatively impact upon her political future. I was disturbed, not just because I believed Obama was the winner and should've been giving his due, but also because I was concerned for Mrs. Clinton's future.

Now all is in the past and we must shape the future. As Francis Bacon once said, "That which is past is gone, and irrevocable; and wise men and women [my addition] have enough to do with things present and to come." I believe Senator Clinton will do all that she can to support Barack Obama.

. . .

WEDNESDAY, AUGUST 27
Bill Clinton's and Joe Biden's Speeches and the Roll Call Vote

THIS MORNING, I DECIDED I WOULD WALK TO THE SHERATON Hotel, located about ten blocks from the Teatro. It was a lovely morning. A slight breeze was blowing. My friends, the mountains, were stark and majestic. I felt invigorated. When I approached the Sheraton, Keith Wright, son of Judge Bruce Wright, was doing an interview with CBS, TV 2. When he was finished, the newscaster came to me to do an interview.

She asked about Hillary Clinton's speech the night before. She asked if I thought Clinton's speech would succeed in creating unity. She also asked about the unity breakfast that was planned for later. I responded, "Mrs. Clinton's speech was super. She said all the right things. I don't know how anybody can doubt her sincerity. She said that she's going to campaign for Barack, and I believe her." The interviewer persisted, "But there are Hillary supporters who say that they cannot back Obama. They say that they will either stay home or vote for McCain." I responded, "The question or problem is no longer centered on Clinton. One of the most important points she made in her speech was that if people supported her because they like her, and for no other reason, they are after a personality cult. But if they supported her because of the issues she enjoined, they should also support whoever enjoins the same issues. In this instance it is Barack Obama." The point she was making was that people should be clear about whether they are endorsing a candidate because of the issues or because of personality.

"It is time that Hillary supporters got out of the sandbox and the milk bottle drinking. The issue is deeper than personal feelings. It has to do with winning the Presidency of the United States of America. It has to do with our future. It has to do with who will appoint the next Supreme Court Justices and who will be making decisions that will affect our grandchildren. It is time to put away childish things and embrace those persons who represent what we want to see happen in the future. If McCain does that, then vote for McCain. If it's Obama, then vote for Obama. It's that simple. Nothing complicated." The interviewer nodded her head. I know not whether the interview was shown on television.

When the interviewer departed, Keith and I reminisced about his father, Judge Bruce Wright. We remembered when the Police Benevolent Association and many white New Yorkers subjected his father to vicious verbal attacks. I had invited Judge Wright to preach the Easter sermon at my church. After the service, we remained in the sanctuary for a press conference to discuss the attacks.

I went to the New York delegation's breakfast in the Sheraton ballroom. Assemblyman Darryl Towns and his father, Congressman Ed Towns, were present. Congressman Towns had given Leah her first job in Washington, as an intern, when Leah was a junior at Dartmouth College. I greeted William Thompson, New York City Comptroller, who introduced me to Kevin Johnson, the former great point guard of the Phoenix Suns, now running for mayor of Sacramento, California. Congressman Charlie Rangel and I sat at the same table. As always, he was very friendly, and the consummate politician. I did another interview with TV5 ... same question and same answer as with TV 2.

Later, I returned to the Colorado Convention Center for the second meeting of the African American Caucus, and I arrived midway during the panel discussion. I was asked to do an interview for the *Final Call* newspaper. The questions asked during the session were wide-ranging. Primarily, the interviewer wanted to know my feelings regarding Leah being the CEO, what Obama's candidacy means for black people, and my thoughts on how far we have come since the Civil Rights Movement and Dr. Martin Luther King Jr.'s 1963 "I have a dream speech."

When I finished the interview, I had missed so much of the panel discussion that I thought it was useless to stay. And, similar to yesterday, there was excitement in the air. Bill Clinton and Joe Biden would speak tonight.

I returned to the hotel, got dressed, and started for the arena. It is as though everybody had the same idea: Let us get to the arena as soon as possible. There were more people and movement on the streets leading towards the arena than before. The inside of the arena was packed early and those who had called requesting a seat in our box had come earlier than at any time before. Reverend Jackson had requested ten seats and all the members of his family were present. In the upstairs box sat Angela Bassett, D.B. Woodside, who played the part of Melvin Williams of the television series on the Temptations; Bishop Blake, my old friend Winston Hill and his wife Carol. In the box downstairs sat Blair Underwood and his family, among others.

As we sat watching the proceedings, I begin to feel a strange excitement. There was a stirring, and accompanying whisperings, indicating that somebody of super importance was around or about to enter. And, sure enough, led and surrounded by several people came Muhammad Ali. Cameras begin to click. Hands begin to clap. And people began to call his name.

It was a profoundly poignant moment. He passed me as he was led to his seat in Leah's box. He was shaking and I knew that he did not recognize me. I didn't even attempt to get his attention. Once he was seated, I went over to him. I said, "The last time we met was in East Orange, NJ. Do you remember? You came to me and asked in a rather defiant tone, 'Can you preach?' And I got in your face responded with equal defiance 'Can you fight?' Shaking your head, and pressing your lips together, you said through your teeth, 'You are a preaching so and so and so…' and we both had a belly laugh." When I finished, I saw an amiable, broad smile across his face and a twinkle in his eyes. It was the only time I saw it that night. It was a light moment for everybody.

After the usual preliminaries, former President William Jefferson Clinton came to the podium. The reception given to him was equal to the one given to his wife. He commenced his speech by saying, *"Last night, Hillary told us, and no uncertain terms, that she is going to do everything she can to elect Barack Obama. That makes two of us. Actually that makes 18 million of us…. Because like Hillary, I want all of you who supported her to vote for Barack Obama in November."* There was thunderous applause. Now Bill Clinton had stated that he categorically supports Obama. He went on to give the reason for his support, *"And here's why I support Obama. And I have the privilege of speaking here, thanks to you, from a perspective that no other American Democrat, except President Carter, can offer. Our nation is in trouble on two fronts. The American dream is under siege at home and America's leadership in the world has been weakened. Middle-class and low-income Americans are hurting, with incomes declining, job losses, poverty and inequality rising, more foreclosures, credit card debt increasing, healthcare coverage disappearing and a very big spike in the cost of food, utilities, and gasoline. Our position in the world has been weakened by too much unilateralism and too little cooperation."* He concluded his speech by urging Democrats to line up behind Obama. He said, *"And so my fellow Democrats, I say to you; Barack Obama is ready to lead America and ready to restore American leadership in the world. Barack Obama is ready to honor the oath and to preserve, protect, and defend the Constitution of the United States."* When he was through, an earthquake-like response seemed to shake the very walls of the arena. It was indeed a high point of the convention.

Following President Clinton was Vice Presidential nominee, Senator Joe Biden. He spoke of his years growing up in poverty and hardship in Scranton, Pennsylvania. He related how his mother encouraged him to be tough. He told the story of coming home after having been beaten up. His mother told him to go back out into the streets and bloody the nose of the person with whom he had been fighting. The crowd received him very well. And in spite of following Bill Clinton, he succeeded in sustaining the high level of enthusiasm and ecstasy

Then came the moment of truth. It was time to vote. Hillary's and Barack's names had both been put on the ballot. As each state was called, the suspense heightened. It had been agreed that Hillary Clinton's name would be on the ballot. This was done to honor her for her great campaign as well as to win over her supporters. When the roll call reached California, California passed. In our box, we wondered why. We knew something was up. And then New Mexico yielded to Illinois and Illinois yielded to New York. There was a hush across the arena. There were quizzical looks on many faces.

Looking down upon the New York delegation, I could see the gathering of Governor Paterson, President Clinton, Comptroller Thompson, Congressman Rangel, Senator Chuck Schumer, Speaker Sheldon Silver, State Senate Minority Leader Malcolm Smith, and in the middle was Hillary Clinton. With the arena now gripped in this strange silence, Senator Clinton got permission from the Chair, U.S. House Speaker Nancy Pelosi, who was presiding over the roll call. Senator Clinton then said, "I move that Senator Obama be voted our choice for President by acclamation." Pelosi put the motion forward. With a thunderous "Yes," the delegates agreed to Mrs. Clinton's motion. The great gathering at the Pepsi Center wrote their names on the pages of history. Those who were blessed to be present shall forever remember the moment.

Later that evening there was a birthday celebration for Leah's 45th birthday. What a birthday present, to be born the day before Dr. King's "I have a dream speech" and to play such a vital part in this night of history. At the party, Chairman Dean spoke of her efficiency, sincerity, and commitment. I spoke of the days of her babyhood through her youth. Concluding, I said, "Leah, you are the fifth generation of preachers in our family. You have set the bar of achievement so high that the next generation will have a towering challenge to match or surpass your accomplishments. God Bless you! You have made the hearts of your parents, your staff, your church, and your community beat with joy and pride."

From the site of the birthday celebration to the hotel was about two blocks. I returned to my hotel walking on a cloud. As I fell asleep, I still remember whispering prayers of gratitude.

THURSDAY, AUGUST 28
The Lead Up to Obama's Speech

WELL, THE DAY HAD ARRIVED. THERE WERE GROWING QUESTIONS that had been agitating my mind ever since I learned that the final night of the convention, when Obama would be speaking, would be moved to Invesco Field. (Most Denver residents prefer that the stadium be referred to as Mile High Stadium as opposed to Invesco Field and they don't mind correcting you when you use Invesco.) A lot of people are required to fill a 76,000-seat stadium. Anything short of that would be viewed as a failure. I know a little bit about the internal tension and I know that it would be hard enough to fill the stadium with a united staff and sufficient time to achieve success. But the event of the evening was light years more important than anyone's feelings. The hopes of countless people, all across the world, were swinging in the balance of what would happen tonight. Plus, if the Clintons could rise above their feelings, who could do less?

I had remained neutral during the primary. I found myself wrestling with a personal dilemma. On one hand were the Clintons, whom I knew in some small ways, along with people I admired who were very close to them. And on the other hand was Obama. I didn't know him, nor did I know the people around him. In addition, Leah's position demanded neutrality from her. And, being her father, I thought I should also remain neutral.

However, I think deep down inside I wanted Obama to win the primary. Not Obama really, but what he represented for people of African ancestry across the world, not just for our time, but also for generations to come. I believe America and the world needs a change. Whiteness has had long years of rulership and blackness needs a chance. But was Obama really the black hope? Or the hope of blackness and whiteness?

Another challenge was the décor for the stadium. The Pepsi Center's set design had already been decided upon and constructed. Now, there had to be plans for the stadium. Several plans had been submitted to Obama's people. They chose the "Greek" motif and there were loud criticisms. Obama's critics argued that the Greek columns looked arrogantly ostentatious and were another manifestation of his "bloated ego".

And on top of all of the above, there was the threat of rain.

As I walked to the Colorado Convention Center, at least one concern was laid to rest as the sun gave promise that it would be triumphant. I felt relieved. There was the usual frenzy of activity, especially today. Everybody wanted tickets for the stadium. I had received calls from different parts of the country and I went to make sure that all of the requested credentials were in order. Afterwards, my wife and I had lunch with the Bishop Charles and Mrs. Blake. It was a delightful lunch with one of the most powerful religious leaders in America. We dined in Peaks Restaurant in the Hyatt, a long, narrow room, surrounded with huge picture windows that allowed a marvelous view of the city and mountains. Reverend Dr. H. Beecher Hicks Jr., pastor of Metropolitan Baptist Church in Washington, D.C., came by for a brief chat. He also ranks among the most influential religious leaders in America.

After lunch, there was a reception for the Faith in Action Committee in Leah's suite. It was supposed to be a time for light refreshments and thank yous. But there were so many urgent matters that had to be addressed that there was little time for anything else.

Important people were still calling for credentials, employing every conceivable strategy. Even as we were leaving the suite for the stadium, calls for credentials were coming in. And there were still problems at the stadium that needed immediate attention.

Two SUVs awaited us downstairs. As we left through the revolving doors, Sharon was still trying to handle credentials and take care of our transportation. We were happy to be able to supply transportation for Dr. Adelaide Sanford and Dr. Sheila Evans-Tranum.

It was a short distance from the hotel to the stadium. But today the security and crowds made it seem miles away. As we drove up to the stadium, long, twisting lines encircled the elevated colossal stadium. As we got closer, the lines seemed even longer. Significantly, there was a feel of patience and excitement in the air. People were polite and saying "excuse me" if they felt they had offended someone near them. It was a good sign. I'd felt the same civility on other occasions (i.e., when the Mandelas came to New York and in some of our demonstrations when we were fighting for a good cause).

The crowd inside the stadium seemed as large as the crowd on the outside. We finally located our suite, after laboriously negotiating the crowd. It was on the fourth level. There were three adjoining boxes, each with panoramic views of the open stadium. We didn't have the best view of the stage from our boxes but we did have comfort, food, beverages, delightful company, and TV sets that showed the happenings on the field. This gave us an option. We could watch the proceedings directly on the field or on TV or both, which is what we did.

I went from box to box, greeting our guests, some of whom had arrived early. Mrs. Michelle Paterson was comfortably seated with her son. Governor Paterson followed her. After a brief chat, he and Michelle departed. On his way out, he asked if Leah had received the birthday flowers he had sent. "I'll ask her," I replied. I thought to myself, how thoughtful it was that with all of the things on his mind, he remembered my daughter's birthday.

Looking across the stadium, I turned my eyes toward the banners that were hung around the top. They had the names and retired numbers of some of the great Bronco football players: Terrell Davis, Karl Mecklenburg, and, of course, the icon, John Elway. It was unreal. Here I was, seated in a highly prized luxury suite, scanning the field of football wars that I had viewed innumerable times on TV, never thinking that I would one day be seated in the luxury boxes with VIPs, waiting for the event of a lifetime—far more important than a football game, waiting for the first African American to accept the Democratic nomination for the President of the United States.

The stadium was slowly filling up and there were still large sections of empty seats across the stadium. I began to get anxious. I must've been the only one because everyone seemed contented and even happy. Everyone all over the stadium was glad to be present. As the evening wore on, the seats were completely filled. The crowd reached a capacity of 84,000. The 76,000 seats had been filled plus extra seats had been placed on the field. By the time Dream Girl, Jennifer Hudson, sang the anthem (and oh how she sang, reminding me of Whitney Houston's performance for the Super Bowl years before) the stadium was nearly filled and people were still streaming in.

There were the usual preliminaries—speakers and music. I liked "Ain't No Stoppin' Us Now," by McFadden and Whitehead; it seemed appropriate. I hoped it was a prediction of things to come.

By 8 pm, the stadium was filled. A video was shown as flashing lights pierced the engulfing dusk. An eerie silence pervaded the stadium. Perhaps people were listening to their heartbeats. Then, stepping out on the stage, between the Greek columns, with adjoining lighted windows behind, was the man of the hour, the one whom the crowd had come to see and hear. The stadium seemed to shake as the crowd let out thunderous screams and loud applause. Off in the distance, the mountains, seemingly recognizing the moment, decided to become smaller. He stood there, looking around, waving his hands, which excited the crowd even more. He was basking in the moment, knowing that it was his moment. His time had come.

Obama's Speech

MY MIND RACED BACK TO 1984, SAN FRANCISCO, CALIFORNIA, the year Jesse Jackson made his move for the Presidency of the United States. It, too, was a great moment. As I'd watched Jesse deliver his stirring speech, I'd felt the same emotion that I was feeling now. We had worked so hard and come so far. But even that didn't compare with this moment. This was unreal! I could continue to try to describe it all, but Kevin Merida, *Washington Post* staff writer, captured the scene and feeling in moving, vivid language with an informative reference to history in an article entitled "For the Descendants of

King's Dream, A New Day Dawns." Let's let him, an objective observer, convey the unforgettable moment. He wrote:

> "No one said this exactly, but imagination was the quiet star of this day, that thing that leaps over walls and moves the fences of out limitations.
>
> Forty-five years ago, many of those who jammed the Mall in Washington to hear a young Baptist preacher exhort the nation to be better were just trying to get the foot off their necks, win the right to vote, stay at a highway motel, and eat at a decent diner. They were trying to send injustice packing. Not elect a black man president. Most had not yet envisioned that.
>
> But imaginations have expanded this campaign season, soaring beyond Invesco Field, where Barack Obama accepted the Democratic Party's nomination Thursday night, becoming the first African American to stand before his nation and ask for its November vote.
>
> As the masses streamed into the Denver Broncos' football stadium and took their seats in the baking afternoon sun, throats tightened and eyes got misty. And old hands shook with nervous excitement. Many had waited three hours to get in, and never considered turning around. There is a saying in the black church: "Your steps are ordered," which is to say your path is preordained, your way set.
>
> Mississippi was one of the scariest states in the nation for blacks at the time. It was not a "Yes We Can" state. It was the second state to secede from the union, a state known for its lynching. It was the state where 14-year-old Emmett Till was brutally murdered and thrown into the Tallahatchie River; a state where three civil rights workers were killed as they

embarked on a voter registration drive a year after he marched on Washington.

On Thursday, the Mississippi delegation took its seats in the back, near the end zone, right behind Utah and in front of the CNN booth.

Mississippi had changed. "You know that old saying? 'The hands that picked cotton can now pick a president,'" said Rep. Bennie Thompson (D-Miss.). This is the state of a thousand Black elected officials; a state that Obama overwhelmingly carried in the primary. The Democratic National Convention wouldn't seat Emma Sanders in 1964, but she is seated now.

When Obama had settled the crowd down, he commenced his speech. He opened with a tribute to Chairman Dean and to Senator Dick Durbin. He expressed gratitude to Bill and Hillary Clinton, Senator Ted Kennedy, Senator Joe Biden and a special salutation to his wife Michelle and daughters Sasha and Malia. "To Chairman Dean and my great friend Dick Durbin, and to all my fellow citizens of this great nation, with profound gratitude and great humility, I accept your nomination for the presidency of the United States." Then he gave a description of the conditions in the U.S.A.:

> "We meet at one of those defining moment. A moment when our nation is at war, our economy is in turmoil, and the American promise has been threatened once more.
>
> Tonight, more Americans are out of work and more are working harder for less.
>
> More of you have lost your homes and even more are watching your home values plummet.
>
> More of you have cars you can't afford to drive, credit card bills you can't afford to pay and tuition that's beyond your reach.

> These challenges are not all of government's making.
>
> But the failure to respond is a direct result of a broken politics in Washington and the failed policies of George W. Bush.
>
> America, we are better than these last eight years. We are better country than this.

He compared the Democrats with the Republicans. Then he laid out his program:

> Unlike John McCain, I will stop giving tax breaks to corporations that ship jobs overseas, and I will start giving them to companies that create good jobs right here in America.
>
> I will eliminate capital gains taxes for the small businesses and the start-ups that will create the high-wage, high-techs jobs of tomorrow.
>
> I will cut taxes for 95% of all working families because in an economy like this, the last thing we should do is raise taxes on the middle-class.
>
> And for the sake of our economy, our security, and the future of our planet, I will set a clear goal as president: in 10 years, we will finally end our dependence on oil from the Middle East....Now is the time to finally meet our moral obligation to provide every child a world-class education, because it will take nothing less to compete in the global economy.

He said what he would do as Commander in Chief:

> As Commander in Chief, I will never hesitate to defend this nation, but I will only send our troops into harm's way with a clear mission and a sacred commitment to give them the equipment they need in battle and the care and benefits they deserved when they come home.

> I will end this war in Iraq responsibly, and finish the fight against al-Qaeda and the Taliban in Afghanistan.
>
> I will rebuild our military to meet future conflicts….Because one of the things that we have to change in our politics is the idea that people cannot disagree without challenging each other's character and patriotism.

He concluded:

> At this moment, in the election, we must pledge once more to march into the future.
>
> Let us keep that promise, that American promise and in the words of Scripture hold firmly, without wavering, to the hope that we confess.
>
> Thank You, God Bless you, and God Bless the United States of America.

Throughout his speech, he was frequently interrupted with applause and yells. On occasion, there was standing ovation. It was a powerful speech! The admiring throngs were not ready to depart from the historic moment. With the candidates, their families standing on the stage, waving and smiling, the huge crowd clapped and screamed and waved back. The fireworks, like a rainbow, were scattered across the sky. There were booming cannon blasts. Confetti drowned the candidates and participants. It was like a 4th of July fireworks in New York City.

Then, it was over. The candidates disappeared behind the Greek columns with their families. The crowds began to smartly leave the stadium. It was amazing that so many people could depart with such order and swiftness.

Afterward, we went to another birthday party for Leah. This was a much smaller gathering of close friends and family. It was held in her suite. Again, Chairman Dean, along with others, lavished praise upon Leah. They spoke of her character, competence and cordiality, a rare blend of admirable qualities.

It had been a long day and now it was over. How quickly the greatest moments passed into oblivion. Perhaps, this is why we humans, since time immemorial, have tried to capture a great moment in stone or literature or film. It is our feeble attempt to add eternal quality to our transient accomplishments.

FRIDAY, AUGUST 29
DNC Meeting

THERE WAS ONE MORE ITEM ON THE CONVENTION'S PROGRAM, the post-Convention meeting of the Democratic National Committee. Usually, the nominees attend and make remarks. However, Senators Obama and Biden did not attend this session. I had been asked to do the invocation. I had also done the invocation following the 1992 Convention in New York City when Clinton and Gore were the nominees.

As I walked the four blocks to the CCC, I was amazed at how few people were in the streets. Just a few hours before, swarms of people crowded the streets, stores, restaurants, and bars. Now, they were all gone. Where did they go? How did they vacate so fast? It reminded me of a passage from the Holy Bible, where it is written, "How does the city sit solitary that was full of people!" The Biblical reference, however, spoke to the destruction brought about by enemies resulting from God's punishment for the sins of the people. Today, though, the city was not empty because of any negative reasons.

When I reached the center, it too was empty. Access was easy. A couple of officers stood at the doors. Yesterday, there were people lined up outside and the security was tight. Inside, hordes of people moved to and fro and/or sat at tables, disseminating literature. Now, they too were all gone.

Without interference, I went straight to the ballroom where the meeting was scheduled to begin at 10:00 am. When Chairman Dean gaveled the meeting to order it was 10:15 am. After Dean introduced me, I thanked Chairman Dean and the DNC members for choosing my daughter to be the CEO of the Convention and giving her unstinting support. I reminded the assemblage of my invocation in 1992 and the victory that followed. Then I prayed.

Oh, Lord our hope in ages past, our help in years to come. Our shelter from the stormy blast and our eternal home. We are profoundly grateful for this moment in history—a moment many of us believed would never come. We are grateful for the memory too, of the dreamer, Dr. Martin Luther King Jr., who always believed that this time would arrive and that we would reach the promised land. How wonderfully strange, indeed, are thou ways, Oh Lord. That, this moment would come on the 45th anniversary of his famous "I Have a Dream" speech in which he predicted this day would come.

We pray for Senators Barack Obama and Joe Biden upon whose shoulders millions of people have placed the heavy mantle of leadership and have put their hopes for a better world. Before them, stretches a campaign trail that can be rocky, tough and negative. We pray for their strength to endure hardness; courage to face the fiery darts of their opponents; the clarity of vision, sharpness of mind, tenderness of spirit; a fair and balanced judgment, that what they say and do will always be consistent with your will. Throw your arms of protection around them and their families.

> Oh Lord, we know that You taught us to always conclude our prayer with "Thy will be done." But You have also taught us to pray for what we desire. Honesty compels us here in this room to declare our desire. And our desire is that the candidates we have chosen will lead us to victory in November.
>
> We pray this prayer, not just for our own gratification, but because we are firm in the conviction that they represent the highest hopes for America, indeed, for the world. Nevertheless, Thy will be done. In Your name we pray. Amen.

After the prayer, the proceedings continued. One highlight was a resolution offered by Don Fowler, a veteran Democratic bigwig and former Chairman of the party. The resolution called for the expression of gratitude for Chairman Howard Dean, Reverend Leah Daughtry, CEO of the convention, and the convention staff. Prior to offering the resolution, he said that of all the Conventions he had attended, this one was the best of them all. Obviously, I was elated on two accounts. Firstly, my daughter had been singled out for a job well done. And secondly, I'd had the honor of doing the invocation. As my wife and I were leaving the center, the departing delegates continued to gather around us with approbation.

With all of the convention responsibilities over, it was my intention to spend the rest of the day traveling to the mountains. The day was warm and clear. Perfect for it. The mountains were majestically visible and seemed to beckon me. However, my plans were soon disrupted when my driver informed me he had been summoned to the carpool. Cars were needed to transport departing delegates to the airport. So I decided I would call Winston Hill and have dinner with him and his wife. He offered to pick my wife and me up at 6 pm.

As I returned to the hotel, I found a penny. Finding pennies always conjures up in my mind my lowest financial point which posed staggering challenges to my marriage and ministry. When Leah was a baby, my wife and I had become virtually bankrupt. Even worse, we were down to our last pennies, 24 cents to be exact. We had run out of food and needed a penny to buy milk for Leah. We searched the house, every pocket in our clothes, pocket books, wallets, and drawers without success. Leah began to cry. Water no longer satisfied her. There was one thing left to do, try to find a penny in the streets.

As I walked and looked, I prayed. I recited promises in the Bible, but I found nothing. Growing weary and frustrated, I decided to swallow my pride and borrow a few cents. A casual acquaintance (I wish I could remember his name) came across my path. I asked him for a loan of a quarter. Smiling, he gladly dropped the coin in my hand. I hastened to the store. I purchased the milk and bought a package of donuts. I couldn't wait to get home and share the good news.

The next day, our fortune changed dramatically. Financial help came from many places and sources. I learned a valuable lesson which I never forgot. This lesson can be summed up in the expression "It is darkest before dawn." Or to put it in theological terms, the devil fights hardest when you're nearest to victory. Or, the devil intensifies the blockage when your blessing is close at hand.

So it seemed appropriate that I should find a penny in Denver. I was reminded that God is faithful. The challenges of life are not meant to defeat us or destroy us, but to strengthen, embolden, instruct and humble us. There are lessons that we learn during times of challenges that we can't learn any other way. These lessons are riveted on our memory.

I will never forget the search for a penny. Whenever I see one in the streets, I put it in an envelope, write the date, time and place where I found it. Now the baby who cried for milk is the Chief of Staff of the Democratic National Committee and the CEO of the Democratic National Committee Convention. She has risen to dazzling heights of achievement.

True to his word, Winston picked us up. But instead of going out for dinner, he brought ribs, potato salad and beans from one of his two restaurants. He didn't know that I was vegetarian. But my wife devoured the victuals. In fact, she took ribs home the next day.

He also drove us to the foot of the mountains, to the site where Buffalo Bill is buried. I purchased a souvenir before we started back to the hotel. Even that short trip was awe-inspiring. We were not the only ones with appreciation for the mountains, long lines of cars were headed to the Stone Giants.

It was enjoyable being with Winston again. He was a great football player during the New York Jets Super Bowl time, playing offensive tackle. I had become unofficial chaplain with the team, conducting Bible studies once a week and providing counseling. Sometimes, I would travel with the team. And other times, I would just be available. From the first day I visited the training camp at Hofstra University (I was taken there by Tom Skinner, the deceased Evangelist), Winston and I became friends. Yes, he was a great football player and an even greater person. He was the key organizer and coordinator of our study sessions as well as anything related to the team.

Well, it became official. McCain picked Alaska Governor Sarah Palin for Vice President. To say it was a shocker is putting it mildly. She's little known outside of the limited conservative circle or state of Alaska.

. . .

SATURDAY, AUGUST 30
Reflections on the Convention

AFTER WE HAD FINISHED PACKING, WE BOARDED A CAB TO THE airport. It was 10 am. I was still amazed by how empty the reception areas, hotel restaurants, and streets were. Perhaps, it just seemed that way because the areas were so crowded just a few days ago.

During the 30-minute ride to the airport, my wife and I discussed the Republican response to the Democratic Convention. I believed they would attempt to do three things:

- Emphasize Obama's reported arrogance and ego mania.
- Say that the Convention was all Hollywood, but no substance.
- Project Governor Palin as the true outsider who would bring change while at the same time subtly pushing the female angle.

Winston Hill met us at the airport. He had brought us some food from his restaurant.

As we flew across the sky, my mind turned back to the Democratic Convention and Governor Palin. I tried to dissect Senator McCain's thinking but I just couldn't understand or follow his line of reasoning. Apparently, I was not the only one; every newspaper I read questioned his decision. One commentator stated, "It is the riskiest political move I had ever seen." I came to the conclusion: it was purely a political move. It wasn't country or patriotism that drove the decision; it was politics. Surely there were other Republicans who were far more qualified. Mitt Romney, for example, former Governor of Massachusetts, would've made a formidable candidate. His economic knowledge and experience would have provided a good balance for McCain's foreign policy expertise. Whatever the reason for McCain choosing Palin, it did succeed in competing with Obama for press and public attention.

My immediate, visceral response to Governor Palin was negative. She impressed me as being brash and brassy. I wondered if I was being chauvinistic but dismissed the thought. There were other women, assertive, "in your face" women that I admired and with whom I had worked on different ventures, Congresswoman Maxine Waters of California; former Congresswoman Cynthia McKinney of Georgia; the deceased former Pennsylvania Secretary of State C. Delores Tucker; and deceased former Brooklyn Congresswoman Shirley Chisholm. These women had depth, sincerity and commitment.

There was something about Governor Palin that exuded arrogance and recklessness, an "I'll get there anyway I can" mentality. Scrappy? Yes. And not beyond employing low blows to win. She seemed capable of using whatever and whomever to get her way. I told my wife, "She reminds me of ball players I played against. They had limited skills but tried to make up for it with intensity and pugnacity. They pushed to the limit the rules and occasionally would go over the line." In the end she's going to do Senator McCain more harm than good." I shrugged my shoulders and whispered that my opinion is based solely upon my emotion, life experience and understanding of human nature. Anyway, time would tell.

We arrived back home at 8:30 pm. The streets seemed darker and the flowers on the stoop had withered. I noticed the mail had piled up. I pulled my bag inside. And, as is as my custom, I immediately started unpacking. Yes, I had returned to reality.

Readjustments always pose a challenge. Coming back to the ordinary, the everyday, after having participated in the spectacular events requires a major effort. It felt as if I had spent time on the mountain top, engaging in history-making events, interacting with movers and shakers, surrounded by magnificent scenery and then returning to the valley to resume the routine. It does help, however, if the valley to which one is returning includes a mission one enjoys.

I remember many years ago when Dr. King, returned to the U.S. after receiving the Nobel Peace Prize in Oslo, Norway. Before heading south, he stopped in New York. The Honorable Robert F. Wagner, Jr., who was Mayor at that time, honored him with a dinner. When King spoke, he thanked everybody for honoring him and supporting his cause. Then he said he loved being in New York. He loved the people and the kindness that had been shown to him. He said that, while he would love to stay on the mountain, the valley calls. He had to go back to Mississippi, to Georgia, to Alabama. He had to go back to the struggles of the south.

Likewise, Jesus took several of his disciples up on a mountain. There, before their eyes, Jesus was transformed into a mysterious, glorious presence. The disciples saw Moses and Elijah with him and they wanted to do what humans do in the presence of ineffable magnificence, nail it down! They said, "Let us build monuments." Jesus, returning to normalcy, rejected the idea, telling them to remember it instead. They had been privilege to see unto the glorious unseen and witness the indescribable beauty of heaven. When they arrived back at the village, they were immediately confronted with a baffling challenge. A young fellow had a demon and/or was acting strangely. Jesus' disciples, whom he had left behind, couldn't do anything about it. Jesus had to take charge.

The Apostle Paul stated his contentment and adjustability. He said "I know how to be hungry and I know to be filled" (Philippians 4:12). It is one of the greatest challenges of life to emulate the Apostle Paul. We should strive to master the external, irrespective of the shape that it takes. Our peace and joy should be within us, deeply rooted within us. Therefore, changing the circumstances and events should not move us from our center.

And so now, home again, I had to make sure the garbage was removed. The sanitation man will be coming tomorrow. Tomorrow, I would return to the church and the community and more exciting adventures. And challenges will continue.

CHAPTER THREE

The General election— Will he make it?

Daily Challenge WEDNESDAY, OCTOBER 1, 2008

FIVE CONCERNS

REP. ELIJAH CUMMINGS (D-MD), CO-CHAIR OF BARACK OBAMA'S campaign, relates a question that was put to him by children. He said, "They come up to me and ask, 'is he going to be okay? Is he going to make it?' Little kids! In many instances they can't even pronounce his name."

I, too, have often been asked, "What will happen in November?" I usually respond that there are five concerns that I have.

■ THE REPUBLICAN "WIN AT ANY COST STRATEGY"

There are three ways that this Republican strategy manifests.

1. **Dirty tricks:** Republican leadership has been known to have no scruples when it comes to winning an election. They are masters of deceit, deception, and misrepresentation. In the last election, the Bush campaign along with the "Swiftboat Vets" impugned the heroism of Senator Kerry. They widely publicized stories that the incident regarding Kerry's heroism in the Swiftboat was not true.

Going back to the Bush/Kerry election of 2004, McCain himself was the victim of lies and misrepresentation. He was accused of fathering an illegitimate black child. The fact of the matter was this: McCain and his wife had adopted a Bangladeshi child whose complexion was dark.

We all remember the Watergate scandal back in the Nixon years. The dirty tricks of Mr. Nixon gained public attention when his campaign workers were caught after breaking and entering into the Democratic headquarters.

The challenge for Mr. Obama is how to respond to this Republican brand of politics. If he doesn't respond, he may be accused of being a coward. Or, people may perceive that the allegations against him are true. Along these lines, there are many who believe that Sen. Kerry's failure to respond to the questions regarding his heroism contributed to his defeat.

If he does respond, he's going to be accused of practicing "politics as usual"—the very politics that he has denounced. It is unlikely he can beat the Republicans in the game of deception, chicanery, and sleaze. I remember when the Police Benevolence Society of New York was harassing Judge Bruce Wright. The media asked him for a response to the scurrilous attacks. He replied, "You can't win a pee pee contest with a skunk."

    2. **Republican thievery:** Republicans have been known to steal an election if at all possible. The case of Al Gore is a classic example. There is no doubt that Gore would've won Florida, and therefore the election, if the votes had been counted fairly. But somehow, with the help of the Supreme Court, Bush emerged as the winner.

    3. **Republican smarts:** The Republicans are not dummies. They have some of the smartest political operatives in the business. It is reported that McCain's top advisors are taken from Bush's office. The McCain camp made a couple of recent moves that underscore my point here. Earlier in the year, Obama decided on a trip abroad. McCain knew that the trip would attract worldwide media attention and requests by the media to accompany Obama. He also knew that there would be crowds of well-wishers in the capitals of the world clamoring to see and hear Obama. McCain would be forgotten in the shuffle. With that in mind the McCain camp had to devise a strategy that would minimize, even ridicule, Obama's trip, while at the same time, maximizing McCain's importance. Toward that end, they did a couple of things:

        A. They criticized the media for giving more time to Obama and demanded the same. They said they were monitoring every second. This made the media nervous. Thus, McCain seemed at times to have gained the lion's share of media attention. Then, they ran ads linking Paris Hilton and Britney Spears to Obama, clearly delivering a message that Obama is a celebrity and should not be taken seriously as a Presidential candidate.

B. Next came the second shrewd move emanating from the McCain camp. During the Democratic National Convention, he kept leaking to the media that he was on the verge of selecting his Vice President. Then, the day after Obama's speech, he announced his Vice Presidential candidate, Governor Sarah Palin. Obviously, she was not the most qualified among the Republican hopefuls. But, none of them would've come close to generating the fan fare she did. This move minimized and distracted attention from the spectacular Democratic Convention, especially Obama's speech. The best Obama could get from the media was shared time with McCain and his Vice Presidential candidate. (As an aside, McCain's selection of Palin was an indisputably political decision, which calls into question his patriotism and love of country as well as "putting the country first.")

■ THE WILLIE HORTON FACTOR

Willie Horton was a convicted felon. while he was on parole, he committed another crime. Governor Michael Dukakis, who was the Democratic nominee and who had been ahead in the polls, was accused of being light on crime and an advocate for parole. This accusation was a contributing factor to his defeat at the hands of George H. W. Bush Sr. in 1988. Again, notice the misrepresentation and questionable tactics. We, then, have every reason to expect that if a black person commits a heinous crime against a white person, the McCain camp would exploit it in the same way.

■ THE RALPH FACTOR

Out of nowhere, Ralph Nader has come back to the scene. He has not been heard of since he derailed the Gore campaign. Vice President Gore would have become President if it were not for Nader. Nader got 90,000 votes in Florida. Gore lost by approximately 500 votes. It is agreed that the overwhelming number of Nader's votes would have gone to Gore. Nader is a pathetic man whose ego seems to have catapulted him into reckless destructive ventures. At one time, he worked on behalf of consumers and was a highly regarded activist. He had even assembled a dedicated staff called "Nader's Raiders." They pursued corporate and governmental fraud, manipulation, and exploitation of consumers relentlessly. Presently, because of his reckless political ventures, rumors are flying that he was paid to get into the campaign.

■ THE MEDIA

Inarguably the media has tremendous influence on the election. It has been said that the media has a love affair with Sen. McCain. During the primaries, there were those who felt that the media favored Obama over Hillary Clinton. Then, there are the conspiracy theorists that believe that the media used Obama to defeat Clinton and will now turn towards John McCain to defeat Obama. They believe it was all a scheme to get McCain elected. Whether that's true or not, time will tell.

■ RACISM

Of course, no one wants to talk about it, not even Obama. For a while, almost nightly, CNN anchor Wolf Blitzer would ask the question, "Why isn't Obama doing better?" almost nightly. Given the fact that the state of the economy and the Iraq war (which the overwhelming majority of Americans disapprove of) are directly attributable to the Republicans who have been in charge for the last eight years, Mr. Obama really ought to be way ahead of Mr. McCain. I often wondered why he kept asking this question. Did he really not know or was he trying to force the race issue on the table? There is no question in my mind that if Mr. Obama was white, plans for the inauguration in Washington D.C. would be under way. The fact of the matter is that no matter what the polls say, once whites go beyond the curtain and vote, no one knows what the outcome will be.

So, those are my concerns. It is unfortunate that there is little or nothing Mr. Obama can do about them. All that he can do is do the best he can, and hopefully it will be enough.

Daily Challenge WEDNESDAY, SEPTEMBER 10, 2008

MCCAIN PLAYS THE PATRIOT, POW, MAVERICK, LOVE OF THE COUNTRY CARDS

REPUBLICAN PRESIDENTIAL NOMINEE SENATOR JOHN MCCAIN delivered his eagerly awaited acceptance speech to raucous, continuously cheering and feet-stomping delegates at the Republican Convention in St. Paul, Minnesota. All during the speech McCain was interrupted with ovations and loud cheers. It was as though the delegates knew in advance, he was going to need a lot of help. One could not help but feel that anything he said would've been met with cheers.

In fact, before he could complete a stumbling, faltering sentence, the crowd was on their feet. I could not help but think if he had been Lucifer coming from the fires of hell and invited them to return with him, the crowd would've been cheering.

It was a dull, vapid, dry, sleep-provoking speech; minus substance, coherency, and passion except when he talked about his imprisonment. Obviously the overwhelming majority of political pundits, all Republican supporters and leaders don't share my assessment of McCain's babblings, euphemistically called speech. Quite the contrary, they were ecstatic with praises for what they called "a great speech". This highlights the wide difference of perspectives in America. Surely, a lot of it, though not all, is related to race or the experience growing out of the racial situation in America. I've often thought that the greatness or absence of greatness of American presidents or leaders should be judged based upon the perceptions of those who occupy the bottom rung of the social ladder. This is the biblical approach towards the evaluation of leadership.

The four political cards McCain played were:

■ THE PATRIOT CARD

Clearly in his speech he was sending a message, I am the most patriotic; I am the most America loving. Across the convention arena signs were held up declaring "Country First." His speech was interrupted with howls of USA!! USA!! USA!! The Republican leadership, known to be robot-like in their approach to everything, obviously had planned to play the patriotic card. The response of Republican leaders to the question of Vice President selection of Governor Palin underscores the point. They responded without answering the questions. They talked about Obama's absence of experience and how great John McCain is. They responded verbatim.

The news people, who have had a long love affair with John McCain, allowed the Republican leaders to get away with the diversion. It was as though the interviewer was asking about apples and the respondents talked about orange and grapefruits. Therefore, it is clear that John McCain is determined to trumpet his patriotism.

■ PRISONER OF WAR CARD

More than ever before, he was long and tear jerking in his relating his prisoner of war experience. He said his record of "scars" proves he can fix what ails the country. It is going to be interesting to see if the American public is going to accept the scars of a prison camp as qualifications for the President of the United States of America. If that is the criterion then every prisoner of war or Purple Hearted veteran ought to get ready to run for the highest office in America.

All due respect, I'm sure most readers will agree with me, there are prisoners of war or Purple Heart recipients we wouldn't trust to lead us through our own places of residence. This is not to suggest that they don't have other skills and talents; it is to say they don't try to capitalize on their prisoner of war experience.

■ THE MAVERICK CARD:

He projected himself as being independent and rebellious. Yet, according to the Democrats, he voted with Bush 90% of the time. His economic policies are typical republicanism, as represented by President Bush for the last eight years and have brought the country to its present economic crisis and credibility gap in the world. As to his claims of bringing change to Washington and America, why, the speakers who proceeded him, especially Governor Palin and, of all people, Rudy Giuliani, were nasty, vitriolic and sarcastic in their presentations. If McCain can't change the behavior and tenor of his Convention how can he change Washington and America? Another aspect that cast suspicion on McCain's claims of being a change agent: just a month ago he was running as the experienced candidate. Now he has seized upon Obama's change strategy and proclaims himself to be the leader of change in America.

■ **THE LOVE OF THE COUNTRY CARD:**
It should be stated that patriotism and love of country qualities should be extolled. This should not be a subject for debate or even discussion. There is suspicion of political motivation when there is an excessive parade of patriotism and love of country. It ought to be assumed that those who run for the presidency of the United States are all patriots and lovers of country. To use patriotism and love of country as a bludgeon to beat up on opponents and/or to blind or intoxicate the American public is wrong and smacks of hypocrisy. I have observed that those leaders who are the most vigorous in encouraging ostentatious display of patriotic symbols, i.e., lapel buttons, flags in windows, bumper stickers, red white and blue underwear, boxer shorts or head rags (not only is it disrespectful but in some places maybe unlawful) have acted contrary to American ideals of equality, justice, caring and concerns for the least in society. Remember Nixon and his men who wore proudly their patriotic lapel buttons. In conservative America, there is an exaggerated parade of patriotism. Among that crowd, it is usually coupled with the Bible. So God and white men leaders or the President of the United States become almost indistinguishable.

The most obnoxious example of exploiting the symbols of God and patriotism or patriotism and God (I'm not sure which one comes first in their minds) are the symbols of a flag and the cross is the Ku Klux Klan.

Mc Cain's selection of Governor Palin raises question of his love of country and judgment. Surely it must've been obvious to all that there were other Republican leaders far more qualified than Governor Palin. How much could he have loved the country when, at 72 years of age, having had three to four serious bouts with cancer, he could pick a person who is a "heartbeat away from the presidency," with absolutely no experience in foreign affairs. Let us remember that for months McCain blasted Obama for the absence of foreign affairs experience. Is there anyone who has any doubt that the decision was motivated by politics and not love of country? Moreover, incredibly, McCain and his assistants had only one serious meeting with Governor Palin a short time before her selection. I cannot help but wonder if McCain decided on marriage after one meeting with Mrs. McCain. The question is, is it his habit to make the weightiest of decisions after one meeting?

After the McCain speech, Democratic leaders, unbiased news analysts and objective observers rushed to point out the absence of substance in the speech. There was no plan put forth to alleviate the economic crisis, the joblessness, the mortgage foreclosure—the issues that according to the polls are number one in America's thinking. But it wasn't about substance, it was about playing the above cards. How well he succeeds, the future will tell. It will be another sad chapter in American history if the American public is deceived or misled by the McCain card-playing skills. If there are other qualities that he has, or programs, or policies or plans to extricate America from its present economic morass and suspicion abroad and to actualize the American ideals, then he ought to win based upon those qualities and not manipulating the emotions of the American people.

Daily Challenge WEDNESDAY, NOVEMBER 5, 2008

REFLECTIONS FROM GEORGIA ON THE OBAMA CAMPAIGN

Dear Reader,

The usual deadline for my Wednesday article is Tuesday at 12:00 noon. However, because of the upcoming election, Monday became my deadline. Both days occurred before the election results. Therefore, this article was written without the benefit of knowing the outcome. However, I thought it would still be of interest to record my thoughts and my feelings on the eve of the election.

It seems right that I should be in southern U.S.A., Augusta, GA as we approach the last days before the Presidential election of 2008. Augusta and Savannah were the cities of my first eleven years. Being in these cities always brings back memories of the dehumanizing system of segregation—separate seating on public transportation, separate water fountains, schools, movies, restaurants, even toilets. The "COLORED" places were always dirty and neglected. The "WHITE" places were clean and well cared for. That was, of course, the idea, a perpetual projection of white superiority and black inferiority.

Driving up the Turpin Hill in Augusta brought back memories of black confinement and immobility. "The Hill," as we called it, was an exclusive, white part of town. Blacks were not allowed up on The Hill after dark. However, during daylight hours, blacks were allowed some freedom. If you were caught on The Hill during the day, it was assumed that the reason for the intrusion was domestic work. This was true throughout most of the South. It was apartheid USA style.

In state houses, city halls, municipal buildings, governmental buildings and places of importance, entrance was denied to blacks, except to work at menial tasks. As our mothers and fathers entered, usually with mops, brooms and buckets, they were forced to enter the back door.

I passed Woolworth (The Five and Dime) while driving along Broad Street. Just as most Broad Streets across America had been in those times, Broad Street in Augusta was a thriving commercial, theater street. But now, along with many of the stores, restaurants, and theaters on the street, Woolworth was boardered up. During those days, Woolworth stores had saturated the USA. As I passed the store, my mind went reeling back to 1965, Greensboro, South Carolina. Three students had decided to sit in the white section of a Woolworth's restaurant. They met the usual fate for their defiance, jail. But, thank God, you can't jail, bottle up, or confine an idea. And, as Victor Hugo wrote, "Nothing is so powerful as an idea whose time has come". The time for resistance had come. Sit-ins, wade-ins, prayer-ins, etc. swept across the country.

We should never forget those experiences. Those of us who lived through them should accept the obligation to keep that part of our history, along with the memories of slavery, alive. Our children, till the end of time, should never forget. For what we have achieved as a people becomes all the more extraordinary when we remember the unprecedented cruelties to which we were subjected. Our history should be a reference point for inspiration, and motivation for our children.

Sometimes I wonder how we, living in the USA, especially in the South, were able, not just to survive, but to make progress. How did we come so far against such formidable enemies? Quite frankly, I can understand it only with reference to God.

Now I am 78 years old. I am 66 years away from the nightmare of my early years in the South, and a black man might become President of the United States of America. Incredible things have already been achieved. There is the Democratic Party nomination; wide acceptance of Obama by whites even in the South; at this point, 138 major newspapers across the country have endorsed him; 84 have endorsed John McCain. At present, he's ahead in most polls. He has raised $150,000,000 in one month.

My mind went back to the 1984 campaign of Jesse Jackson. I was in Savannah, GA campaigning with a developer name Ben Polote. He was one of Jesse's earliest supporters. The night before the election, I could barely sleep. I tossed and turned. Was it real? Were black people really allowed to vote where whites once lived and blacks had experienced limited mobility? I was staying on 46th Street, not far from the polling place that was located on Victory Drive and Bullock Street. It was near where I grew up.

Early in the morning, I eagerly headed to the streets. There was a long line at the polling place and people were still coming. Pride overwhelmed me. That time has a special importance in history. In spite of those who try to minimize or reject it, it remains of paramount significance. In fact, it paved the way for Obama. Minus Jackson and others who went before and after him, there would be no Obama. Indisputably, the campaign of Barack Obama far surpasses the Jackson campaign.

There are those who cannot fully grasp what the Obama campaign means to those of us who have lived through the awful times to which I've alluded. And I am sympathetic to those persons. CNN carried the story of a 106-year old woman. She had lived through many terrible times in American history. But now, she could not wait to vote. In fact, she did vote. It was the crowning moment of her life. I believe I'm within the mark when I say, for most of us, we never believed that we would live to see a black man come this close to being President. During Obama's campaign for many of us, it was as if we were living in a dream. Sometimes, I stared at the television programs, the all-day news channels, trying to absorb it all, while always remembering the South of my youth.

While I was an integral part of the Jackson campaign from the beginning, as I've stated before, I wasn't involved in the Obama campaign during the primaries. I sought to maintain neutrality because Leah, my daughter, held a position that demanded it of her. However, I did significantly contribute vicariously to the campaign and help to propel it forward through my children, especially Leah, who was the CEO of the Convention in Denver. The Convention was, by unanimous accounts, one of the best, if not the best. If the Convention had been a failure, Obama may not have recuperated. But, thank God, the Convention was like jet propellers or boosters. It sent Obama into the political stratosphere.

I know not what will happen on Tuesday November 4, 2008. But, as I prayed at the Executive Session of the Democratic Convention:

> *Oh Lord, we know that You taught us to always conclude our prayer with "Thy will be done." But You have also taught us to pray for what we desire. Honesty compels us here in this room to declare our desire. And our desire is that the candidates we have chosen will lead us to victory in November.*
>
> *We pray this prayer, not just for our own gratification, but because we are firm in the conviction that they represent the highest hopes for America, indeed, for the world. Nevertheless, Thy will be done. In Your name we pray. Amen.*

My prayer becomes even more fervent when I remember the sordid, scurrilous campaign waged by Senator McCain and Governor Palin. The attacks have been relentless. Obama has been called or it has been suggested that he is a terrorist, anti-Semitic, socialist, un-American, un-patriotic, "THAT

ONE." Senator McCain and his campaign have resurrected the worst passions in American history. Congressman John Lewis was right when he said that the rhetoric of Senator McCain and Governor Palin have created a climate where references to Obama such as "Kill Him" and/or "Terrorist" have been heard in their rallies. And as for "socialist," it is questionable whether or not people know what socialism is. These rallies are every bit similar to the rallies of Governor George Wallace and others who sowed seeds of hatred, bigotry, distrust, and divisiveness.

McCain and Governor Palin are scary people. Decency, fairness and true patriotism demand that they be rejected. While we do not know what Obama's Presidency will produce, we can say that it will be a new day with a promise of better times at home and abroad. With all the emphasis I can command, I say to all who can vote, YOU MUST VOTE. Let it not be said, that in this defining moment in history, there was no participation.

CHAPTER FOUR

Obama, Thank God! Election Day, November 4, 2008

Daily Challenge WEEKEND EDITION, NOVEMBER 7-9, 2008
MORE THOUGHTS ABOUT THE SOUTH

THEY MUST BE ECSTATIC. SOMEWHERE UP THERE OR OUT THERE. The framers of the Amendments of the Constitution must be ecstatic! The 13th Amendment abolished slavery. The 14th conferred citizenship. And, the 15th gave the right to vote. Frederick Douglass, Harriet Tubman, Sojourner Truth, Rev. Henry Highland Garnet, Bishop McNeil Turner, Ida B. Wells,

A. Philip Randolph and the Pullman Porters, Medgar Evers, Roy Wilkins and the National Association for the Advancement of Colored People (NAACP), James Farmer, Floyd McKissick and the Congress of Racial Equality (CORE), Walter White, Whitney Young, and the Urban League, Kwame Toure, James Forman and Student Nonviolent Coordinating Committee (SNCC), Fannie Lou Hamer, Aaron Henry and the Mississippi Freedom Democratic Party, Bob Moses and the students of the Mississippi Summer Project, Michael Schwerner, Andrew Goodman, James Chaney, Ella Baker, Malcolm X, Dr. Martin Luther King Jr. and the Southern Leadership Conference (SCLC)—all who gave their lives for freedom and who understood that the right to vote, to participate in the electoral process was of supreme importance, somewhere, they must be ecstatic.

I started writing this article with a prayer of Thanksgiving. I saw the fingerprints of God all over Obama and his campaign. In an article I wrote in this paper on February 28, 2008, I raised the question that there was something uncanny, strange, and mysterious about Obama and his campaign. I tried hard not to invoke the name of God. I'm always reluctant to interpret human events with reference to God. However, there was no rational explanation for Obama's success. I'm even more convinced now that there was divine intervention. Even Obama, in his victory speech said, "I was never the likeliest candidate for this office. We didn't start with much money or many endorsements. Our campaign was not hatched in the halls of Washington. It began in the backyards of Des Moines and the living rooms of Concord and the front porches of Charleston." The Bible teaches that God chooses the weak, the foolish, the things that the world rejects to effectuate his purpose that no flesh should glory in His presence. And yet in some sense, he was the likeliest candidate. His mixed parentage, his having lived in Indonesia, Honolulu, New York and Chicago, his educational background and community organizing gave him a unique perspective on the world and the capacity to interact with all personality types. Indeed, he was far more qualified to deal with a diverse world than the other candidates. His brilliant mind, steady demeanor, balanced judgment, imaginative visions, even temperament provided a special preparation. He was far more qualified to deal with a diverse world than the other candidates. When a man or woman and a moment meet, earth-shaking, world-changing developments occur. I believe that during those times, it is God who consummates the marriage. The Bible says, "To everything there is a season, and a time to every purpose under heaven...." Still, it is so unreal to me.

Last week, I touched on my growing up in southern USA. I wrote about laws and customs that prevented blacks from going into white parts of town except for employment. Black people had to enter governmental and important buildings through the back door, usually with mops, brooms and buckets. Now in the White House, the most important building in America, a black man will enter, not with mops and brooms but with a mandate from over 52 million diverse Americans to be their leader, the President of the United States.

I wrote about segregated transportation. Black people were forced to sit in the back and even had to give up the backseat for a white person (even a white child) if seating in the front was filled to capacity. Significantly, the height of hypocrisy took place in Washington, D.C., the nation's capital. Going from North to South, blacks had to change seating on the public transportation to accommodate the South. Imagine traveling with your family. You reached Washington, D.C. and you had to disembark. Then, you were herded to the rear that was dirty and neglected. And this occurred in the capital of a nation that prided itself on being the land of the free and the home of the brave. Could there be anything more humiliating? To avoid this humiliation, when black people drove

South they picked their stops. If they stopped in the wrong place, they would face humiliation or death. You were served only in the back, usually through some kind of opening in a wall or a door. And now, it is mind boggling that a black man will ride and be in charge of the most prized means of transportation in the world, Air Force One.

When I went South on my honeymoon, 46 years ago, we stopped at a Dairy Queen in North Carolina. I went to the front of the store and ordered two thick shakes. My wife and I loved the thick, creamy liquid. The young fellow behind the counter looked me straight in the eye and through his teeth demanded, "Nigger, go in the back!" I looked at him for a long time, debating whether I should depart or express my rage in physical terms. I looked back at my wife seated in the car and decided that the better part of wisdom would be to take my anger and return to the car. I thought that if I had acted the way I wanted to act, it would only have exacerbated the situation. I would be killed or jailed. Quite frankly, I think I was prepared for that. But what would happen to my wife? And what agony would this bring to our family? Returning to the car, I continued to head southward, burning with rage. It is likely that my experience, and worse, was duplicated countless time for countless people all across the south.

Moreover, it has been reported that during World War Two German soldiers, against whom America was fighting, could ride up front in public transportation while the black American soldiers who fought against them were forced to ride in the back. During the First World War, President Woodrow Wilson told the American people that they were fighting to save the world for democracy. Perhaps they were saving democracy in the world, but they were not saving the democracy in the USA. U.S armed forces were segregated. It was unbelievable how African Americans soldiers were treated. The condition in which they were forced to live along with the equipment with which they trained and fought with was horrible. The world knows about the Black Eagles of Tuskegee. They were trained with inadequate, outdated, makeshift airplanes. Yet, in spite of everything, when they were put into battle, they never lost a bomber.

I was in the army in 1950, during the Korean War. Although the armed forces were supposed to be desegregated at that time, the physical, and to a degree the social, vestiges of segregation yet remained. While I was at the ordinance school in the Aberdeen Proving Ground in Maryland, I witnessed the places and conditions under which black soldiers were forced to live. I saw the barracks (living places), mess halls (dining areas), training grounds, service clubs (hangout places), and commissaries (stores). I thought about our fathers and brothers who fought gallantly. Some were wounded and some were killed in every war this nation has ever had. So to be treated this way was in explicable. Tears filled my eyes as anger filled my heart. What kind of people were these who could treat their own people so terribly? These were American soldiers and employees. These were people who were fighting and dying to protect America. They were working to make life better for Americans and their loyalty and dependability were without question.

When orders came for me to ship out to Korea, I was given a few days' leave. Along route 54, just outside of the camp, there was a train station. I had to use the toilet before catching the train homeward bound. I hurriedly ran into the train station's diner but was stopped at the door. My plea to use only the restroom (I knew I could not eat in the diner) was angrily rejected. I stood there, trembling with rage. Here I was (sharp as a tack) in my uniform, brass sparkling and combat boots shining, and I was prohibited from using a toilet. I reflected later that I really didn't want to kill anyone. But, if I had to kill, why go thousands of miles away? The person upon whom I ought to direct my rifle was down the road from the camp, in a diner. I decided that Uncle Sam and I needed a divorce. I sometimes think of my friend, Isaac Lavine (we called him Stitch), who like countless other soldiers, went to Korea and never came back. William Lavine, Stitch's big brother, was the greatest wide receiver the Jersey City Vikings ever had. Maybe, the man in the diner was doing me a favor. Maybe his treatment of me was God's will. Who knows?!? I may never have come back from the battles of Korea.

After all of my experiences with the Armed Forces, it is incredible to ponder the present reality. The Commander and Chief of the United States Armed Forces is a person of African ancestry. Is there any wonder why I discern the fingerprint of God in all of this?

Daily Challenge WEEKEND EDITION,
NOVEMBER 14-16, 2008

ELECTION DAY MORNING

AFTER TOSSING ON MY BED THROUGH THE NIGHT, I WAS GLAD to see the morning arrive. I was eager to get to the polling place. I thought 6 am would be early enough. In the past, voting had always been a quick exercise. This day, although it didn't seem that long, it took an hour. It was an unseasonably warm morning with a slight dampness, hinting that rain might be on the way. However, the sun was triumphant. Perhaps the sun wanted to celebrate too.

There was pervasive cordiality on the line. Everybody was giggly, giddy, and gabby. Small talk on smiling faces and laughing lips could be heard and seen up and down the queue. Everybody greeted each other as though they were long-lost friends. Indeed, everybody wanted to be friendly, to share the moment. History was being made and people were relishing it, wanting to prolong it, wanting to engage others in it.

I didn't hear one complaint regarding the length of the line. A sense of pride vanquished all complaints and discomforts. There was a couple ahead of me who spoke of chiding youths who were complaining about the long voting lines. "You stand on line all day and night to see a rock star. This is far more important," they said to the listeners, who nodded their approval.

There is a phenomenon I have observed among people who are engaged in a worthwhile cause: they are respectful, courteous, and helpful. For example, there was a feeling of pride, joy, and respect during the time that Nelson Mandela visited New York. Likewise, this feeling has permeated many of the demonstrations that I have led. Significantly, it was reported that there was not one incident among the thousands who gathered to hear Obama's speech on November 4th. (I wonder if anyone has done a study of the crime rate during the time of great movements, i.e., Civil Rights Movement, Black Power, etc.?)

I met Spike Lee as I neared the door. He was exiting, on his way to Chicago for Obama's celebration. We greeted each other with hugs. "The great Reverend Daughtry," he said. "The great filmmaker, Spike Lee," I responded. "It's a great day," he declared. Raising his camera, he said, "Let me take your picture." "I'm honored. Maybe there is another *Mo' Better Blues* in the making," I said, referring to his movie. (I'd had a cameo part in the film, performing the marriage ceremony between Denzel Washington's and Joie Lee's characters.)

As I returned to my place in the line, a blind man passed by with a stick in hand. Using it like an antenna, he tapped the steps and along the fence to the sidewalk, smiling all the way. A courtly middle-aged woman led him. There were other elderly, and physically challenged people there, all exuding pride and joy. Three fourths of the people on the line appeared to be of African ancestry. And almost half seemed to be middle aged or younger. Many had children with them.

Along came a tall sister with a male companion. She was smiling and singing an upbeat cheering song. Her high-pitched voice could be heard before she came into view. Everybody along the line smiled and nodded at each other. She captured the feeling of the people. We all wanted to sing with her but fear of embarrassment held the tongues of 90% of the people on the line.

When I entered the school (the polling place), a woman with an authoritative voice was barking directions. I entered the auditorium where the voting booths were. It was filled to capacity. Immediately, a couple of persons complained to me about a voting machine that did not work. I gave them directions on whom to call. I approached the desk for my district and gave my name. After identifying my name in the book, I signed and was directed to the appropriate booth. Entering the booth I studied the names before me. I was looking for one name: Obama. After finding it, I scanned the many names beneath it. I recognized several of them and decided I would vote for them too. I stood alone before the lever, wanting to treasure the moment. I offered a prayer of thanksgiving and pulled back the lever, removing all that had gone before. I pushed down the little lever under which Barack Obama's name appeared, then pulled the lever back and hoped my vote was recorded. If it wasn't, I'll never know. I will always believe that it was. Thus I, like millions of others, had exercised one of the prized opportunities of this nation. I had participated in history.

I learned later that others who had entered the booth had their own rituals. They carried pictures of ancestors, or relics and or heirlooms, or took pictures of themselves in the booth. Everyone paused to savor the moment.

Returning to my car, I passed the line that had now lengthened considerably. The demeanor of the people had not changed. They were still smiling, chatting, laughing and enjoying their walk into history.

Daily Challenge MONDAY, NOVEMBER 17, 2008

ELECTION DAY AFTERNOON

WHEN I RETURNED TO THE CHURCH, I BEGAN TO PREPARE FOR an interview with CBS-2. They had called the previous day to arrange an interview. They'd also asked me to organize a group of people to be interviewed regarding their feelings on this day. I carefully selected an assortment of persons of varying ages and genders. When Channel 2 arrived, I was interviewed by Maurice DuBois in the Sanctuary. He asked me what I was feeling. As has become my custom, I rehearsed the history of my growing up the segregated South. I expressed how I never believed this day would ever happen. I was grateful that God had allowed me to see it.

After we finished, we joined the others who were waiting downstairs in the Fellowship Hall. There was Mrs. Gwendolyn Wilson, age 78, a long-time member of my church and Chair of Alonzo Daughtry Memorial Day Care Centers, of which there are currently three. There was also Mrs. Lila Brown, age 77, also a long-time member; Mrs. Christine Holeman, founder of our church's usher board; Jerry King, secretary of Alonzo Daughtry Family Life Services; my wife, Dr. Karen Daughtry; and Ms. Ayana Vincent, Executive Assistant for Downtown Brooklyn Neighborhood Alliance (DBNA), 1st generation from Grenada, one of my favorite places. (Grenada always conjures up the memory of the New JEWEL Movement, particularly its president Maurice Bishop.)

It was a profoundly moving interview. We sat together in a semicircle. Mrs. Wilson expressed concern regarding the Bradley effect (Tom Bradley was the mayor of Los Angeles who was expected to win his race; all of the polls had him far ahead. However, he lost. Many people believe it was because white people said one thing to the pollsters and did another thing when they were in the privacy of the polling booth.) When asked if she had voted, Mrs. Holeman said "No," and then explained that when she started for the polling place, a neighbor informed her that the lines were long. She decided to return to her home, get a chair and vote later. She was overcome with joy that she had lived to see this day. Her voice faltered and she could barely be heard.

Mrs. Brown spoke of Dr. King's dream being fulfilled. Dr. Karen Smith Daughtry also echoed Dr. King, referencing the check that Dr. King had said came back from the bank marked insufficient funds. Dr. Karen said that the check now was certified. And then, Ayana stated that once this experience was over she would finally be able to breathe. When the interview was complete, the camera crew took pictures of historic events and personalities that saturated the walls and tables of our church.

As the day progressed, I tried to make a decision about where I would spend the evening. I called Councilman Charles Barron and he informed me that he and others planned to convene at The Poli (short for Political) Café in East New York. We had celebrated the victory of his wife, Inez, in her run for the 40th Assembly District Seat at this same site. I thought about joining them there. I also thought about going to Harlem, which seemed an appropriate place to be. But I finally decided that I would just stay home—I knew it would be an astounding victory and I wanted the moment to myself.

I asked Charles if he thought that Obama would win it. He was emphatic in his belief that Obama would be victorious.

I said, "I believe he's going to win, but I'm still uneasy. Do you think the Republicans will steal it?" He replied, "I don't know what will happen. But if they try to steal it, there will be a revolution." We laughed about it and he said "Take your pick. Obama or Revolution?" I never returned an answer.

I decided to leave a bit early so that I could get home by about 4 pm. As I walked the streets and went into the various places of business, people were waving and smiling and talking about the election. There was a feel of anxiety, anticipation, pride and joy. The greetings took on a consistent form: "Did you vote yet?" It was a given that everybody was voting; it was just a matter of when. Then inevitably there was a discussion about the length of the lines, with everybody saying that the lines were longer than they'd ever seen.

Daily Challenge WEDNESDAY, NOVEMBER 19, 2008

ELECTION DAY EVENING

IT WAS AROUND 4:30 PM WHEN I ARRIVED HOME. I MADE MYself comfortable. I knew I would be home for the rest of the night. I sat by the bed, glued to the television set and waited for the returns. Occasionally, anxiety got the upper hand over my faith. I wondered and worried that something would or could go wrong, even now. On September 10, 2008, I had written an article in this paper, expressing my concern that the Republican Party's "Do Anything to Win Strategy" would succeed in stealing the election. Would the fact that they had saturated the television with negative ads in the last couple of days sway the American public? Would the people who were the primary base of Obama's campaign (i.e., youth and African Americans) show up at the polls on Election Day? Youth have a history of absenteeism. Similarly, black people only voted 60% in the last election. Would the Latino vote go for Obama? Would the Bradley effect enter the polling booths? Would there be any gaffe by Obama or Biden? Would black people commit some heinous crime or foolish act that would influence white voters?

It is interesting to note how we took heed to ourselves that we say or do nothing that would negatively impact the campaign. I would study the people behind Obama as he spoke. I was concerned that they would act inappropriately or there would be too many of us. Two memories came to mind. I remembered when I was asked to sit behind a leading speaker at the 2004 Democratic Convention. We were given serious instructions on how we should sit, look, act, and what we should wear. Secondly, I remember how careful Jesse Jackson was about the scene behind him. There had to be diverse representation. On one occasion, we went to a Chicago White Sox baseball game. Before the game started, Jesse was invited onto the field to greet the players. As we got up and headed toward the field, the black security entourage encircled us. Jesse stopped abruptly. Shaking his head and pointing his fingers, he said "No, no, no. You all go back. Just Daughtry and I are going on the field." As we walked onto the field he whispered to me "Man, we don't want all those stern looking black men around us. White folks would think we coming to take over."

Roland Martin, radio and CNN commentator, stated that black people were cautioning him not to be too aggressive and not to speak out of turn about Obama. "Don't make the white folks too angry" somebody said. Murphy's law states "If anything can go wrong, it will go wrong." Could anything go wrong at this late date?

I pondered calling my high-profile friends to urge them to become invisible. I had tried to make myself scarce and to employ caution with my verbiage. The treatment of Dr. Jeremiah Wright should be a lesson to all of us. They tried with all their might, up until the last hours of the last day, to derail Obama's campaign by replaying the Reverend Wright video. I felt we could not risk being misrepresented, misinterpreted, and misused as a pretext to besmirched and or derail the campaign.

As I studied the crowd in Grant Park, Chicago the television cameras focused upon a couple of faces. Rev. Jesse Jackson was shown repeatedly with tears in his eyes and his face contorted. It was hard for me to discern if he was crying for joy, sadness, pride, or for penance. Joy for the victory of Barack Obama; sadness for all those who suffered and died to make this moment possible; pride for what had been accomplished and even for his own contributions; or, penance for his recent remarks regarding what he would do to Obama.

Significantly, I came across a book written by Bob Faw, entitled *Thunder in America* published by the Texas Monthly Press. The book captures parts of Jackson '84 Presidential run. In the book, I'm quoted expressing my concern regarding Jesse's habit of talking too much. During the campaign, I was often asked to talk to Jesse about his use of improper language. Those around were embarrassed and tried to discourage the vulgarity. Among a private gathering of persons Jesse believed to be confidants, he was reported as having made an offhand statement about his going to "Hymietown" (meaning New York). It almost derailed his campaign.

In the same book, I made reference to Jesse's use of profanity. I remember how badly I felt that the author had recorded my remarks. Now, looking back, maybe it was a good thing. What it shows is that some of us were trying very hard to prevent what we knew would keep him in trouble. It's a melancholy consideration that the same loose lips that got him in trouble in 1984, got him in trouble in 2008. So today, rather than being honored and appreciated for his years of struggle and contribution, he is the object of criticism and condemnation. And it appears that even Obama has distanced himself from him. It almost makes me want to cry. I know firsthand, from my years of travel and association with Jesse, of his contributions, his struggles, his sacrifices, and his agony.

Another face in the crowd was Oprah Winfrey. Oprah was crying too. She was leaning on the shoulders of a hefty Caucasian. It raised eyebrows. I don't know if the interest was more in Oprah's crying or the man upon whose shoulders she was leaning. It was later revealed that he was just a stranger.

And the third face I saw in the crowd was my daughter, Leah. I wondered how she was doing. It was my observation that the campaign had not treated her fairly nor given her credit for what she had done at the Convention. I made notes to send her an email, which I did later.

Maybe it's just a father's exaggerated concern about his daughter. I think I speak on behalf of all fathers when I say that when our children are mistreated, it is time for war. And it really doesn't matter whether those who victimized them are kings, popes, or presidents. In fact, I criticized the black press. I did not think that they had given adequate recognition. So again, maybe it was all a figure of my imagination. (See "Open Letter to the Black Press").

Daily Challenge WEEKEND EDITION,
NOVEMBER 21 – 23, 2008

ELECTION DAY RESULTS

RESULTS BEGAN TO COME IN AS SOON AS THE FIRST POLLS CLOSED at 7:00 pm. First, it was Kentucky, McCain was leading. The first good news was Obama winning New Hampshire, a state McCain had banked on winning. Everybody was waiting for the returns from three major states: Florida, Ohio, and Pennsylvania. And, of course Virginia and North Carolina were key. If Obama won those, it would show a trend that would almost guarantee victory.

Then came a major piece of good news. Pennsylvania had gone for Obama. McCain had tried hard to win Pennsylvania and any hope of his winning the election rested upon on Pennsylvania. I began to breathe a little easier. Then along came Ohio and Florida and I knew that it was all over. By 11 pm the news reporter said, "It is over. Barack Obama is the next president of the United State of America."

I stared a long time as tears welled up my eyes. I felt the goose bumps and my mind was flooded with images of people who gave their lives struggling for the vote. I rehearsed the history of the transatlantic slave trade. I studied the crowds, the thousands who had gathered in Chicago. It was a fascinating diversity: the young and the old, the men and women, boys and girls, Asians, Latinos, Native Americans, the physically challenged and I would guess gays and straights. They were all there!

When Obama started his speech, I looked at my watch. It was 11:55 pm. He spoke about 15 minutes, which took us into the next day. I thought to myself, there is something symbolic about this. He starts one day and as he speaks, a new day dawns. Perhaps it signifies that we have moved into the dawning of new time, a new day and hopefully a better day.

I stayed up long into the night, thinking, flipping the channels, and watching the crowd's reaction. It seemed that in every part of the globe, people were celebrating. In America, particularly in black America, the best reference I have or the most realistic comparison I can make is the black community's reaction to a Joe Louis' victory. I don't know if there was any "dancing on the ceiling," to cite Lionel Richie's song, but there was certainly dancing in the street. We hugged, we cried, we jumped. We screamed and found something to beat. (Drums are such an essential part of our history. Rhythm is in our blood, it's in our melanin. The sound and rhythm flow from our connectedness to the vibrations of the universe. We have to beat something. When I was growing up in the churches, there were those who could make music on a wash board or wash tub. And of course we know of the steel drums of the Caribbean. The Rappers' beat and lyrics, sometimes corrupted and commercialized, flow from this history.)

I heard two criticisms regarding the event. One was about Michelle Obama's attire. According to some, "It was a disaster." Others said, "She was making a bold statement." Whatever she was wearing, it does seem to this non-expert on fashion that she didn't need to have that dress on for this occasion. The second criticism concerned the speech. There were those who wondered why Obama did not mention Dr. King's name when he paraphrased lines from the "I Have a Dream" speech. They wondered if the absence of Dr. King's name was a Freudian slip or a clear message that just as he had left Dr. King's name out of his speech, he was going to leave a lot of black folks out of his plans. This leads into the next question, how is Obama going to relate to people of African ancestry?

In an article I wrote for this paper, I raised questions, regarding Obama's background and associations. I stated that I did not know him, nor did I know anyone who was really close to him, except Dr. Jeremiah Wright. Most of the people whom I knew, who had any kind of relationship with him, were not enamored with him. From the beginning, there were widespread questions raised about his blackness. Did he really have black consciousness or awareness and how would he relate to the black community?

After the election, I had heard people say, "It's not about black and white anymore; it's about fixing things." White America, almost unanimously, extolled this "monumental achievement." "A glorious country," they said. "No other place in the world like it." Some of the commentators were beside themselves. They couldn't find superlatives adequate enough to express their unrestrained joy and pride. The general feeling, uttered or unexpressed, was that racism was dead. We were now living in a "Postracial America. Long Live America!" But is that true and what can we look forward to?

Firstly, racism is very much alive embedded in the traditions and structures of American society. Not even a black man elected to the Presidency can dig deep enough to eradicate the centuries-held belief, deeply rooted in Euro-American consciousness and lifestyles. In fact, a very real danger exists now: we could witness an eradication of programs and policies that were designed to redress centuries of cruelty and discrimination. These programs and policies were put in place to enable blacks and other minorities to achieve equal status. "After all, we've got a black President now, what more do we need to do?" would be the reaction of many whites.

Secondly, racism that exists within structures can continue even while those who work in and sit on top of the structures are denouncing racism. Structural racism means that corporations have built-in controls which give rise to and reinforce white advancement and privilege. It's not seen. It is not recorded. It's not written. But it is there. White privilege isn't going to disappear with a black President. In my book, *My Beloved Community*, I quote authors Columbus Salley and Ronald Behm who wrote in their book *Your God is Too White:* "Maintenance of the basic racial controls is now less dependent upon specific discriminatory decisions and acts. Such behavior has become so well institutionalized that the individual generally does not have to exercise a choice to operate in a racist manner. The rules and procedures of the large organizations have already pre-structured the choice. The individual only has to conform to the operating norms of the organization, and the institution will do the discriminating for him."

It may require at least one or two or more generations

before racism is completely removed from minds, structures and traditions. However, the fact that Obama won the youth vote gives us a bit of hope. These young people will be glad, indeed proud, to testify to their children and grandchildren that they supported an African American for President.

But what of Obama? I have been discussing racism in the white community. What can we expect from the Obama administration? I am forced to say "We're going to have to wait and see." I confess my hopes are not too high that he is going to put black people at the top of his agenda. If there is anything for us at all, it will be because we are in a crowd with other people for whom he wants to do something. Except for his grassroots organizing in New York and Chicago, I wish I could cite something else in his background and/or associations that would enhance my hope for substantial change. Maybe there are those who can give other reasons. If they're out there, I certainly hope they hurry with some answers.

Now does this mean we should be without hope? Or can we expect nothing to come from all our adulation, support and prayers? Indeed, much will come of it. We will reap the benefit of this election for generations to come. And this may be, in spite of Obama. He is a symbol. Symbolism is powerful, perhaps more powerful than the reality it represents. The very fact that across the world an image of blackness is going forth that will inspire millions is super-important. In my travels around the world, I've seen, especially in Europe on television, on posters, in literature, images of black people that were grotesque and degrading. There were images that I saw, especially of some of the rappers, that were nauseating. But now, there is the image of a proud, brilliant, dignified, confident, handsome black man who is President of the United States of America. Now, black children yet unborn can aspire for the highest office of the land. Yes, boundless is the benefit of the symbol. And from this symbol, countless men, women, boys and girls will be inspired to achieve in all the fields or professions of the world.

Yes, celebrate the symbol while critically analyzing the substance. Be active in the movement, while holding accountable the man. Simply put, there are four "P" categories we should observe analyze and study:

- **PERSONNEL**: Who is he appointing and for what position?
- **PRIORITIES**: What is at the top of his concerns?
- **POLICIES**: What policies is he formulating and projecting?
- **PROGRAMS**: What programs are being planned?

To repeat: rejoice, celebrate, and be active, for all of us have contributed to this moment.

CHAPTER FIVE

A Week to be Remembered: January 14-21, 2009

Daily Challenge WEDNESDAY, JANUARY 28, 2009

JANUARY 14-16: MEETINGS WITH SEVERAL GROUPS IN NEW YORK CITY

DURING THE WEEK OF JANUARY 14-21, 2009, THERE WERE TWO names on everybody's minds and lips. Countless pages of print media had stories from every conceivable angle. The electronic media were constantly flooded with images of the two men. Talk shows, news stories, docudramas, documentaries, analyses, and interpretations abounded. Even the families were brought into the stories and pictures. And, wonder of wonders, the two men are men of African ancestry: a civil rights leader and the first African American President of the United States. An unprecedented event will occur the day after the national holiday honoring the Civil Rights leader. Even the holiday is a first. It is the first time a private citizen has been honored with a national holiday.

During this week of firsts, I too was carried along with the mania, enjoying every minute of it. In the next several articles, I will share some of my experiences, starting with my speaking engagement for the Environmental Protection Agency (EPA) on January 14th, and concluding in Washington, D.C. with the change of the leadership at the Democratic National Committee (DNC).

Wednesday January 14th 2009: Environmental Protection Agency

ON WEDNESDAY JANUARY 14TH, I WAS A FEATURED SPEAKER FOR the EPA, located at 250 Broadway (see Daily Challenge article in the Appendix). This federal office building sits atop the African Burial Ground. The Burial Ground encompasses huge areas of downtown Manhattan where over 20,000 Africans were buried. This building also houses the offices of the National Parks Department which has responsibility for the administration of the Burial Ground. Behind the gigantic building is a park that includes a monument to the ancestors in the Burial Ground. The bones of over 400 Africans are representative of the thousands. These remains were re-interred in October 2003, after a symbolic journey starting at Howard University and ending in NYC with stops at historic sites connected with slavery.

From the time of our discovery of the Burial Ground in 1991, we fought long and hard to stop excavation and to preserve at least portions of it for a perpetual memorial to our ancestors. I was one of the first to go down into the ground where I viewed the remains of some of our ancestors. It was an unforgettable experience. What I saw, and my emotions at the time, will be with me forever. We tried to change the name of the building from "The Ted Weiss Federal Building" to "The Frederick Douglass Federal Building" We had nothing against Congressman Weiss. We felt, however, that it was incongruent to have the building, which sits atop the African Burial ground, named after a person who was not of African ancestry.

So, this was one of the few times I had visited the building when I wasn't there to confront and/or educate regarding the Burial Ground. I should add that after the site had been made into a National Monument and some of our demands were met, we began to have cordial relationships with the administration. While I didn't plan it, I thought later that starting this historic week at the Burial Ground felt right and proper. I considered our history at this time: from the African Burial Ground and the unspeakable cruelty and suffering of the transatlantic slave trade; to the Presidency of the United States, where a son of Africa, maybe, more directly, a son of ancestors interred in the burial ground, would be sworn in. The life and death of Dr. Martin Luther King Jr. was representative of the long bloody struggle in between. It all seemed divinely orchestrated. (To add another piece to this series of events, I was born on January 13, 1931, during the time of the Depression. Significantly, many people feel we are experiencing a similar crisis.) My grandson, Lorenzo, accompanied me to the program.

Another first, Ms. Lisa Jackson, an African American woman, was appointed to head the EPA. In fact, hearings on her confirmation were proceeding as I entered the building.

Thursday, january 15, 2009: Citibank Dialogue/NRLAA Meeting

I WAS INVITED TO PARTICIPATE IN A CITIBANK "DIALOGUE" convened by Eric Eve, Citibank's Senior Vice President of Global Community Relations, on Thursday from 9 to10:30 am. The purpose of the meeting was to explore ways that CitiBank might address the financial crisis and mortgage foreclosures in particular. The meeting was held at Restoration Corporation Plaza.

It was a walk down memory lane for me. I remembered when the buildings that now house Restoration Corporation Plaza were a milk bottling company. I remembered when Eric Eve was a little fellow. On two occasions, I had organized a bus full of parishioners to campaign for his father, Arthur Eve, who was an Assemblyman and was running for the Mayoral seat in Buffalo, New York. In fact, I spent the final week before the election in his home as we campaigned across the city. Arthur, who was also Deputy Speaker, won the democratic primary, which should've guaranteed victory. But racism in Buffalo refused to allow it to happen. Another man, running on an independent ticket, was elected.

I believe on his birthday, Dr. King would've been somewhere addressing the economic crisis, in particular mortgage foreclosure.

On January 15th, the actual birthday of Dr. Martin Luther King Jr., the National Religious Leaders of African Ancestry (NRLAA) had its weekly meeting from 12 to 2 pm. NRLAA was founded in September 2006 to call attention to the crisis in Darfur, to marshal in material support, and to advocate for peace and humanitarian aid.

It seemed strangely appropriate that in the midst of all the hoopla around Dr. King and President-elect Barack Obama, Africa should be included—especially Darfur, Western Sudan. Since 2003, 200,000-500,000 people have been killed there and two and half million have been displaced. The United Nations has called it one of the worst humanitarian crises in the world today.

In July of 2008, the Special Prosecutor of the International Criminal Court, Luis Moreno Ocompo, issued an indictment of the Sudanese President, Omar El-Bashir, charging him with genocide, war crimes, and crimes against humanity. The three-judge court is expected to issue a warrant for Bashir's arrest.

Surely, Dr. King, were he alive, would be deeply concerned about Darfur. And Mr. Obama has expressed a determination to put an end to the genocide, employing whatever means necessary. So, on January the 15, during NRLAA's weekly meeting, we dealt with issues related to Darfur, but we also took special time to include the life and times of MLK Jr. and the Presidency of Obama in our discussion.

Friday, January 16, 2009: Revival Conclusion

OUR ANNUAL PRAYER REVIVAL IS ANOTHER SIGNIFICANT DEvelopment during this historic week that I feel compelled to include. Historically, the church has had celebrations in great moments of our history. When Abraham Lincoln issued the Emancipation Proclamation in January 1863, the

Bridge Street AME Church (then located on Duffield Street, Downtown Brooklyn, where Polytechnic University now owns the building) had a three-day celebration, commencing with the December 31st watch night service. Again, while we did not plan this prayer service with Dr. King's birthday and the Obama Inauguration in mind, it is, nevertheless, historically appropriate that churches should have celebrations. Our prayer revival included our petitions about the President elect, and throughout the evening, there were constant references to the events surrounding Obama's Presidency and great hope for the future. It was a time of prayer and celebration.

Daily Challenge WEEKEND EDITION,
JANUARY 30-FEBRUARY 1, 2009

JANUARY 17-18:
NAACP AND CHURCH MEETINGS
Saturday, January 17, 2009: NAACP

ON SATURDAY, JANUARY 17TH, AT THE ANNUAL DR. MARTIN Luther King Jr. (Dr. MLK Jr.) breakfast of the NAACP of Jersey City, New Jersey, before hundreds of well-dressed attendees packed into the Grand Ballroom of the Newark, NJ Airport Marriott, I was honored to receive the annual Dr. MLK Jr. award. I have received many, almost annually, Dr. MLK Jr. awards. This one, however, at this time, had a special meaning. I've always treasured any Dr. MLK Jr. award, given by anybody or any organization, anytime—so high is my admiration and appreciation for the man. As I was connected to him in life, I still feel connected in death and the awards help to substantiate the mystic union.

Kabili Tayari, Deputy Mayor of Jersey City and President of the NAACP, a ranking radical from the heydays of the Black Power Movement, an old friend and sometimes foe, gave me the award. Back in November 2008, my wife Dr. Karen gave the keynote address at the Annual Freedom Fund. The NAACP had honored both my wife and me in the last several months. This represented a family commitment or a keeping of the family commitment. My family has produced at least five generations of religious leaders. There has always been the belief in the family that we have a covenant with God. If we lived right, struggling with and for the people, God would make our lives meaningful and purposeful. All of our children are pursuing service-oriented careers. And finally, this award, coming three days after the birth date of Dr. King, which will be celebrated nationally on January 19, 2009, the day before the swearing in of the first African American President, had a deeper meaning and a feeling no words can describe.

In the sociopolitical area, January, especially this January, is the birth of Dr. MLK Jr. We should be perpetually grateful and joyful for his life, for he meant so much, to so many, for so long.

Among the dignitaries present were Jeremiah T. Healy, Mayor of Jersey City; Councilwoman Viola Richardson; and Senator Sandra B. Cunningham, wife of the deceased Mayor Glen Cunningham, first black Mayor of Jersey City. Her presence added another meaning. Glen's older brother, Lowell, and I were friends. Glen was always race conscious, sincere, and committed to advancing the rights, equality, and dignity of our people. He too, worked hard to make this day possible.

• • •

Sunday, January 18: Remembering Dr. King in Churches

AS USUAL, I PREACHED BOTH THE 8 AM AND 12 NOON WORSHIP services at my church. I continued a theme I had started at the beginning of the year: "Joy in January". This theme followed another theme I started in December of 2008, a "Covenant with the Creator." While I didn't plan it, it seemed natural to follow a theme that emphasized the faithfulness of God to deliver on His promises, with a theme emphasizing joy.

Stress, anxiety, worry, fear, depression, and despondency should no longer occupy or control the life of the believer. For God hath not given us a spirit of fear; but of power, and of love, and of a sound mind. (1 Timothy 1:7). Happiness should be the center, the foundation of our lives when we believe in the promises of God.

In addition to the joy surrounding Dr. King's birthday, the Swearing-In of President-elect Barack Obama should enhance the joy this January. After worship, two of my assisting ministers (Bro. Linwood Smith and Bro. Cuyler Cohen), started our journey to the North Shelton African Methodist Episcopal Church in Piscataway, NJ, where I was scheduled to preach at their annual Dr. MLK Jr. Ceremony.

It had begun snowing as we drove. As we listened to the radio, the Philadelphia Eagles, one of my favorite football teams, were losing to the Arizona Cardinals in the playoff game, NFC Championship. It was the only downer over the weekend. The Eagles eventually lost. There was some consolation, however, from the football world. The Pittsburgh Steelers, with its first-year black coach, Mike Tomlin, beat the Baltimore Ravens to win the AFC Championship. This game was more important than the Eagles' game. I always root for black coaches. I feel like a traitor when I attempt doing otherwise.

North Shelton AME is a newly built, circular church pastored by an old friend, Rev. Dr. Kenneth L. Saunders. From the crowded parking lot, we knew the program was well attended. Inside the beautiful sanctuary, our assessment proved to be accurate. Even the pulpit was lined with ministers. In my presentation, I continued the theme, "Living the Dream," from my speech at the Environmental Protection Agency (see the Appendix). By way of introduction, I added several criticisms. I criticized Obama for not choosing a black minister for the invocation. I believe that had it not been for black preachers, there would be no black President. The black church has, from the beginning of our struggle for freedom, been in the vanguard. I reminded them of what W.E.B. DuBois stated, as quoted on page 5 in my book *My Beloved Community*:

> It was a terrific social revolution, and yet some traces were retained of the former group life, and the chief remaining institution was the Priest or Medicine man. He early appeared on the plantation and found his function as the healer of the sick, the interpreter of the unknown, the comforter of the sorrowing, the supernatural avenger of wrong, and the one who rudely but picturesquely expressed the longing, disappointment, and resentment of a stolen and oppressed people. Thus, as bard, physician, judge, and priest, within the narrow limits allowed by the slave system, rose the Negro preacher and under him the first Afro-American Institution, the Negro church.

Moreover, Obama will be sworn in the day after the national holiday honoring Dr. King. The invocation was a marvelous opportunity to educate the world regarding the history of the black church, and to pay a debt for all that the grand old church has done.

Second, I expressed my criticism of Obama's graciously offering forgiveness to his old foes, including Senators McCain, Joe Lieberman, and Hillary Clinton, which was a good thing to do. But, a similar grace has not been extended to Reverends Jesse Jackson and Jeremiah Wright. Why?

And finally, I was critical of those who say that Dr. King's dreams have been fulfilled: that race is a dead issue. Would to God it were true, for then all of us could rejoice and shout the victory. The reality is, and we must face the harsh truth, racism is not dead. Personal relationships may have improved significantly, but racism is deeper than liking your neighbor. Racism is a worldview. It's a tradition. It's a way of life. It's a custom and it is deeply embedded in the systems and institutions of America. No first-time black President, even if he or she is fully conscious, proud of race and accomplishments, committed to promoting black interests (which doesn't fit the description of Obama), would be able to end racism. It may require another two or three or at least one generation. From the response, I concluded that the majority of the audience agreed with me, although not enthusiastically.

It should be noted that in the audience was Ms. Millie Scott, the first black freeholder in Middlesex County, NJ

Daily Challenge WEDNESDAY, FEBRUARY 4, 2009

JANUARY 19:
THE BROOKLYN STEPPERS

IT WAS 9:10 AM WHEN I ARRIVED AT THE SPRAWLING RED BRICK building that housed Boys and Girls High School in Brooklyn. Parents and youth were disembarking buses and cars and hastening into the school. Two members of my church, Mrs. Evangeline Umpthery and her talented daughter, Samantha, met me at the door. Samantha, nicknamed "Little" because of her size, plays the cymbals in the percussion section of the Brooklyn Steppers.

I was guided into the gym where staff and youth were scurrying about, packing and unpacking, arranging and re-arranging, and organizing, while energetically chatting and chewing on gum, donuts, and candies. It was a youthful beehive of activity. Excitement and energy were palpable.

There were still cameras, TV cameras, and newspeople doing interviews. Proud parents and guardians, some of whom serve on the Parental Advisory Board, were in clusters across the gym and moving to and fro, guiding and instructing their children.

The Brooklyn Steppers, ages 8-21, were organized around 1988 by the deceased Mr. Zeke Clemins, Mr. Paul Chandler, and Mr. Tyrone Brown. They were formerly a part of the Jackie Robinson Athletic Club. When they branched "off" in 2004 to form the Brooklyn Steppers, Tyrone Brown maintained his position as director. He is assisted by horn instructor Glen Davis, and Desmond Hill, assistant to Mr. Brown and drum instructor.

There are about 200 kids in the band. Criteria for acceptance into the band includes keeping up grades in school. Members of the band have to show Mr. Brown their report cards. 101 members of the band will be traveling to Washington, D.C. for the Presidential Inauguration. They will take four buses, two for staff and parents, and two for students. Their colors are maroon, white, and yellow.

The group is already widely renowned and the invitation to perform in the Inaugural parade only added to their fame. Their future invites include: Atlanta, GA, Jamaica, West Indies, New Orleans, LA; Warren Country, NC, and Senegal, Africa for the 2009 Fesman International Festival.

After the completion of the equipment check, and a review of the schedule, the band went upstairs to the cafeteria for a continental breakfast. Upstairs, there were more parents, some of whom I knew. There were also children whose parents I had known years ago. I met Tendai Watkis, the daughter of Baba Yusef Imam, deceased cultural revolutionary. He was chief of security when I chaired the National Black United Front (NBUF). I also met Mosunmola Coard and Ajale Coard, the daughter and granddaughter of Mama Kuumba, respectively.

Meeting these people and being in Boys and Girls High on Fulton Street, which was a main street during the days of my youth, sent me down memory lane. I had spent so many years walking and playing on this street. And, on this Dr. MLK Jr. birthday and the eve of the swearing-in of the first black President, a thousand memories flooded my mind.

At about 9:40 am, Mr. Brown called everyone to order with a blow on his whistle. He told us to form a circle with the parents standing behind the children. Then, he gave his last instructions. "Gather your belongings and board the buses immediately. First stop, Madison Square Garden, then Washington. Dunbar High School will provide housing. The world will be watching. Be on your best behavior." Then, he introduced me. First, I commended Mr. Brown, his staff, and the youth. I said, "You all have made us feel very proud. This is a great honor you have received. You will be telling your grandchildren about it. So enjoy and savor the moment." I prayed that God would protect them and raise their prodigious talents to the highest level.

Throughout the morning there was a wonderful feeling in the midst of the excited, vivacious, playful youth. I smiled to myself as I remembered the words of Mark Twain: "Youth is a wonderful thing. Too bad it has to be wasted on young people." On a more serious note, I wondered if the youth really understood and appreciated this moment in history and the privilege given to them to participate.

They reminded me of the Mo' Better Jaguar Football Program. There were three teams arranged in ages 8-15. Coaches Chris LeGree and Irving Robinson founded the program. In 2001, they won the Pop Warner National Championship in Orlando, Florida. I was the spiritual advisor to the program for several years. It was a great program and I loved being with the hundreds of kids and their families. Many of the kids went on to college, where they continued to play football. In fact, for some, a football scholarship was the only way they could enter the school.

When I see and/or hear the negative images so often projected of our youth, I think of these two programs. And of course, there are many, many others positive programs across the city and nation.

After spending the rest of the day at church, I boarded the 7:55 pm Amtrak train and arrived at 11:45 pm in Union Station, Washington, D.C. It was windy and bitterly cold. But even old man winter, huffing and puffing, couldn't keep the people off the buses, trains, cars, and streets. A large part of Union Station was closed off because Vice President Elect Biden was having a party there. Once outside, train passengers had to scurry around to flag taxis. Usually, after waiting in a line, A Union Station worker directed you to a waiting taxi. However, tonight, order and courtesy disappeared as everyone jumped in any taxi, even if they had to jump ahead of waiting customers. Human survival or comfort seemed to reveal how thin the veneers of the niceties of civilizations really are.

Once I arrived at my daughter's home, I settled in for the night or what was left of it. My daughter, Leah, gave me instructions. "We will be meeting our party later this morning at 6:30 am." It was now after 1 am. The early time didn't matter; I didn't think I would be doing much sleeping anyway.

• • •

Daily Challenge WEEKEND EDITION, FEBRUARY 6-8, 2009

JANUARY 20: BEFORE THE SWEARING IN

IT WAS 6:15 AM, WHEN LEAH, RENNIE, AND I, HIT THE STREETS. My grandson Rennie had arrived earlier in the morning. It seemed to have gotten colder. Nevertheless, the streets were already crowded. People wrapped in all kinds of clothing were moving purposefully, laughing, and talking. They didn't seem to mind the cold weather, nor the jostling and pushing. There seemed to have been one thing on their minds—getting to the mall.

Buses were lined up around our house. Riders were stepping briskly from their vehicles, following the directions of yelling leaders. There were persons being wheeled about in wheelchairs. Early on, the predominance of youth became conspicuous and it would be so throughout the day.

Our destination was about 20-25 blocks away. Ordinarily, it is a brisk 20-25 minutes walk. But this morning, we were uncertain about how long it would take. A few blocks away, we headed down the stairs to the Metro (Washington's Subway/Train system) and it was too crowded. On both sides of the steps, people were pushing their way upward. It was clear we would have to walk.

All along the way, masses of humanity, seemingly increasing every minute and with every step we took slowed down our pace. Plus, there was pushing and shoving, forcing us to dodge through the crowd.

It was 7:15 am when we succeeded in arriving at our destination which was C and First Streets, on the corner where the Cannon Building and in the House of Representatives office complex stands. When all of the members of our party arrived, we walked down First Street and entered the Rayburn Building, named after the powerful, deceased Texas Congressman. As was the order of the day, it was crowded everywhere, inside and out. Obviously, it was much more comfortable inside.

Our party included members of the Winans family; veteran civil rights struggler, political organizer and executive, Rev. Willie Barrow; Denzel Washington, Halle Berry; etc. While we waited, I walked over to the smiling actress. I had been very critical of her nudity in the movie for which she won an Oscar. But, she was so pleasant, and of course, so very pretty, that my criticism melted away. I asked her if she would take a picture with me. She smiled the cutest smile you ever did see, and said, "Yes, Reverend. Of course, I will be glad to." And she won herself another admirer.

There is a lesson here. Being cordial, friendly, and humble, can quiet your critics and might even disarm or win over your foes. I'm reminded of a story that is told about the wind and sun. They were having an argument about which of them was the most powerful and persuasive in getting people to do what they wished them to do. They picked a man tightly wrapped in an overcoat. The wind blew and blew, and the man hugged his coat to himself even tighter. The sun laughingly waited for the wind to exhaust its efforts. Then, the sun began to turn on its charm. It became warmer and warmer and the man began to loosen his coat, until finally he took it off. The moral of the story is obvious. In some instances, you can gain more with a smile than with a storm.

After going through the security checkpoints and showing our tickets inside and outside, we found ourselves outside of the building. We crossed the street and were in the park adjacent to the area in front of the Capitol building, where the ceremony would take place. We found our section, which was colored orange. The terrain was divided in colors and numbers, green, yellow, orange, maroon, and blue. Off in the distance, the silver-colored section was reserved for standing areas. Each section was roped off. Our section was about twenty rows back, directly in front of the semicircular VIP section, where sat governmental officials. We had a good view of the podium where the President would be sworn in and make his speech.

It was about 9:30 am when we settled into our seats. I looked around and there were masses of humanity everywhere. Looking backward, toward the obelisk-shaped Washington Monument, people, like ants, were crowded into both sides of the fenced off areas, and the crowd was increasing with every second. A collage of colors and various body shapes, constant movements and conversations, broke the cold and clear monotony.

There were children everywhere, in arms, riding on shoulders, in carriages, and walking or standing hand in hand. Everybody was on his or her best behavior. "Excuse me" and "Beg your pardon" seemed to be on everybody's lips, even when no wrong had been done. Smiles were on all faces. I began to wonder if the smiles were frozen. Even as the sun was beginning to shine, it could not chase away old man winter. Cameras were everywhere, clicking constantly. It seemed everybody had a camera but me.

There was one act that threatened to bash the camaraderie. When people remained standing, there were screams from the rear, "Sit down!" The screams grew louder and angrier as standees remained standing. Eventually, the shouters won out.

With layers upon layers of clothing, feet and hand warmers (they really worked!) a wool knitted hat pulled over my ears, and a Brooklyn Stepper maroon baseball cap given to me by Ms. Umpthery, I sat comfortably, huddled in my top coat which was buttoned to the top, observing, analyzing, praying, and digging deep into my memory. It was hard to believe all of this was happening. I thought about all the freedom fighters before my time and those deceased fighters with whom

I had struggled alongside, as well as the contemporaries—all had fought so long and so hard for this moment.

I especially tried to see the countless, nameless faces that had marched with me for the last 50 years. Reverend Al Sharpton has paid me a high compliment on a number of occasions. He has said that just as Dr. MLK Jr. organized masses of people, primarily in the South; I have been the primary, consistent organizer of the masses in the Northeast. These masses gave out flyers, made telephone calls, sent faxes, emails, and many other things that may have been considered small or meaningless. Some simply provided with their presence. They never asked for anything, but gave so much.

Daily Challenge WEDNESDAY, FEBRUARY 11, 2009

JANUARY 20: BEFORE THE SWEARING IN

I REMEMBERED GROWING UP IN GEORGIA, THE DAILY HUMILIAtions, "Nigger get to the back," and "We don't serve niggers here." I remembered the whites-only signs, the grotesque black statues, and the figurines that stood in practically all white people's houses and lawns; the degrading, disparaging depiction of blacks in movies, magazines, newspapers and even in church literature and artwork. The same demeaning of black folks prevailed even overseas. And then there was the violence, subtle and blatant, especially the lynchings, a moderate form of crucifixion—I reflected on the limited dreams and fettered aspirations imposed upon the minds of our people and particularly our children. Thanks, in some small measure to Obama, and the people who elected him, a lot of it is gone now, at least in its blatant forms and manifestations. But, most of all, thanks be to God, who made it all possible—I do believe.

I tried to recall how many times I had been to Washington

promoting various causes. I had missed the 1963 march for aforementioned reasons. But I was there against the wall in Vietnam, El Salvador, Iraq, and to free South Africa. I was there for the Million Man Marches and in 2005, I walked from Brooklyn to Washington D.C. to emphasize health issues. I was there for civil rights issues, reparations, and police misconduct. Mr. Eric Holder, recently appointed Attorney General, was the focus of one of our demonstrations in 1999. He was the Assistant Attorney General to Attorney General Janet Reno. During his time, an unarmed African immigrant was killed in his vestibule in a hail of 50 bullets, fired by four NYC police officers. The jury acquitted the officers. Under the leadership of Rev. Sharpton, mass demonstrations were organized and daily civil disobedience took place at the NYC Police Headquarters. Almost 1,500 people were arrested, including some of the most celebrated artists, athletes, community activists, and elected officials. We wanted the federal government to indict the officers on the violation of Amadou Diallo's civil rights. In 2001, the Justice Department announced that it would not pursue the federal Civil Rights charges against the acquitted officers. Mr. Holder, who was acting Attorney General, said "They could not prove beyond a reasonable doubt that the officers willfully deprived Mr. Diallo of his constitutional right to be free from the use of unreasonable force." If the killing of an unarmed man by four police officers who turn the innocent man's vestibule into a "death chamber" for no logical, rational reason, does not constitute a violation of freedom of mobility; if that is the view of Mr. Holder, (he might have been echoing the government's line. He might do differently, now that he is the chief) then we should not entertain high hopes that anything is going to substantially change in the police abuse of power in the black communities.

After a prelude by the United States Marine Band, the ceremony began with a call to order and welcoming remarks by the Honorable Dianne Feinstein, United States Senator from California. Dignitaries were introduced as they emerged from the Capitol tunnel. As Obama came forward, a deafening roar reverberated across the mall. One observer said that Obama coming out of the tunnel reminded him of our ancestors being taken along the passage from Goree Island on to the slave ships. There were huge television screens scattered across the terrain and port-a- potties were strategically placed.

Reverend Dr. Rick Warren followed with an invocation. Aretha Franklin sang "America the Beautiful." By her own admission, it was not one of her best performances. I'm in total agreement. (By the way, she received rave reviews for her hat!) The Honorable John Paul Stevens, Associate Supreme Court Justice, administered the oath of office for the Vice President. A musical selection of cello, clarinet, piano, and violin required one to have sincere music appreciation in order to appreciate and understand why this selection, at this time.

And then came the moment. It was 12:04 pm. With his wife, Michelle, holding the bible used by President Abraham Lincoln, and his two daughters, Malia and Sasha, standing close by, the Honorable John G. Roberts Jr., Chief Justice of the Supreme Court of the United States administered the Presidential Oath of Office and Barack H. Obama became the 44th President of the United States of America and the first person of African ancestry to hold the office. (Because Justice Roberts stumbled over some of the words, and to blunt all questions regarding the legality of the oath, the two men repeated the oath the next day at the White House.)

On my right side sat my grandson, Lorenzo, a 19-year-old college sophomore, who left the classroom for this occasion. At the completion of the swearing in, we embraced; my left fist, a symbol of power emanating from the black power movement of the '60's, jutted forcibly and victoriously to the sky, this time, I think, more vigorously than ever before. Here was another first. I am right handed; usually it is my right fist that goes into the air. But with my right arm around my grandson, I was forced to use my left arm. Perhaps, it was meant to be so. This unbelievable first demanded a different, or a first kind of response.

It was all so unreal. Was it, "Just my imagination running away with me?' But no. Surely my eyes were not deceiving me, and the bitter cold reminded me constantly. This was real.

My daughter, Reverend Leah D. Daughtry, added to the meaning of the day, significantly. She had arranged our choice seats. I have already mentioned that 45 years before, when she was born on the day before the march on Washington and the "I Have a Dream Speech," I was in a dilemma. Should I go to Washington or stay home with my family? I decided to stay home. So, I missed being in Washington, D.C. in 1963. Now here we were, seated about 20 rows from the momentous proceedings, while millions stood behind and around us. Relatively speaking, few were in front of us—all because of my daughter.

There were other events she would have arranged for us to attend if I had requested. Throughout the years she has held various governmental posts, including: Assistant Secretary of Labor during the Clinton Presidency; Chief of Staff of the 2008 Democratic National Committee for eight years, and Chief Executive Officer of the Democratic National Committee Convention in Denver, Colorado. All along the way she did all she could to enhance our community and to make our family, indeed our people, proud of her.

. . .

Daily Challenge WEEKEND EDITION,
FEBRUARY 13-15, 2009

JANUARY 20: THE SWEARING IN

CONCLUSION

AFTER THE SWEARING IN, PRESIDENT OBAMA COMMENCED HIS speech. It was hard to sustain concentration. The whole thing was too overpowering. After the speech, some of the pundits dissected his presentation. They said, "It wasn't a great speech." "There were no memorable phrases," "No lasting lines." I wondered if old man winter had frozen their auditory nerves; or if the expectations were too high or wrongly directed. In any event, I begged to differ. While Obama was unable to hit a rhythmic cadence, (but neither was Aretha) I thought the speech contained substantive and even poetic phrases and I think Obama made his point.

He urged the nation to choose "Hope over fear, unity of purpose over conflict and discord." He challenged the country to move forward, "Our time of standing pat, of protecting narrow interests and putting off unpleasant decisions—that time has surely passed.... Starting today, we must pick ourselves up, dust ourselves off and begin the work of rebuilding America."

He stretched out his hand to embrace the Muslim world. He said, "To the Muslim world, we seek a new way forward, based on mutual interest and mutual respect." But, he sternly warned, "To those leaders around the globe who seek to sow conflict, or blame their society's ills on the West—know that your people will judge you on what you can build not what you destroy. To those who claim power through corruption and deceit and the silencing of dissent, know that you're on the wrong side of history, but that we will extend a hand if you're willing to unclench your fist."

He called for a political truce in Washington D.C. to end "the petty grievances and false promises, recriminations and worn-out dogmas, that far too long have strangled our politics."

He challenged all Americans to engage in rebuilding the nation by renewing the traditions of honesty, fair play, hard work, tolerance, loyalty, and patriotism. "What is required of us now is a new era of responsibility, a recognition on the part of every American, that we have duties to ourselves, our nation, and the world, duties that we do not grudgingly accept but rather seize gladly, firm in the knowledge that there is nothing so satisfying to the spirit, so defining of our character, than giving our all to a difficult task."

After the speech, I really felt sorry for the next participants because the mass of humanity started moving toward the exits and the johns. Ms. Elizabeth Alexander read a poem she had composed for the occasion. And Rev. Dr. Joseph E. Lowery did the benediction. The Rev., always eloquent, poetic, and humorous, succeeded in significantly staying the crowd's movement. This was probably due to a mixture of reverence and humor. He concluded the benediction by employing an old ditty that has been in the black community for as long as I can remember. He said, "Lord...we ask you to help us work for that day when black will not be asked to get back, when brown can stick around...when yellow will be mellow... when the red man can get ahead, man; when white will embrace what is right. Let all those who do justice and love mercy say, amen."

Finally, United States Navy Band Sea Chanters played the National Anthem. People put forth their best effort, trying to be patriotic. They would walk a few paces and stop, put their hands on their hearts or salute, and then move some more.

Really, they were forced to move, whether they wanted to or not, by the pushing crowd. And then there were biological imperatives, which forced people to make their way to the port-a-potties.

Getting back to the house was more difficult than getting to the mall. The streets were blocked as the President and entourage moved through the city. Also, ambulance sirens meant that somewhere there were sicknesses or accidents. At one point, the mass of humanity was so thick, that there was an unmovable jam-up, a pedestrian gridlock. Only with maximum force and determination were we able to break through. Rennie's size, 240 lbs, and his football prowess, got us through the crowd. But, through it all, amazingly, the crowd remained calm and friendly, even smiling in most instances.

It was 1:30 pm when we arrived back at Leah's home. We watched the parade, led by the President and First Lady, on television. On two occasions, they got out of the new super modern presidential vehicle, called the "Beast", and walked short distances, waving and greeting the crowd. The newscasters commented about how relieved they were and how the security people were relieved even more so, when the President and First Lady returned to the car.

I find it interesting to do a comparison between Fidel Castro and the Presidents of the United States (there have been eleven Presidents since Castro came to power). In Cuba, which is supposed to be a closed society, where people are supposedly very dissatisfied and resent Fidel Castro, he walks around and stands in crowds with very limited security. At times, it seems as if he has no security at all. And when there are people who surround him, there is doubt about whether they are security or staff.

After the President with his entourage had reached the Presidential viewing box, 13,000 participants marched the 1.7 miles, past the viewing stands. A newscaster commented that one-third of the people in the viewing stands were people of color. The most moving act in the parade was a passenger bus, a replica of the buses used in Montgomery, Alabama—a reminder of the bus boycott in 1955, which initiated the Civil Rights Movement and catapulted Dr. King into leadership and immortality. I also caught a brief glimpse of the Brooklyn Steppers.

In the evening, the President and First Lady danced the night away at presidential balls and the after party at the White House. So, by nightfall, after a brief sacred moment at the Capitol building, the sanctity and solemnity had dissipated into the usual swirling bodies, excessive consumption of food and drink, loud music, and raucous voices, which goes by the name of "party" or if you prefer a more dignified name, "presidential ball." How quickly we go from the sublime to the silly.

They say it's my old-fashioned religious upbringing. But I believe that great moments that are suffused with spirituality or divinity, major celebrations, should be religious, with an emphasis on thanksgiving and praises to God.

Moreover, the partygoers are usually people who are present just to *party*. Often, they have done little or nothing to make the accomplishment possible. They are the rich, famous, powerful, and/or connected and/or professional partygoers. Often times they're arrogant, vain, and conceited; all of which, to repeat, spoils or desecrates a sacred moment. I know that I am in the minority, but I would have preferred for the President and the First Lady to go home after the parade, and spend the time together in prayer, thanksgiving, and preparation for the monumental tasks that lie ahead.

. . .

Daily Challenge WEDNESDAY, FEBRUARY 18, 2009

JANUARY 21
THE NATIONAL PRAYER SERVICE

I ATTENDED TWO OTHER EVENTS. THE FIRST WAS THE PRAYER Breakfast at the Washington National Cathedral, which was a 20-minute drive away from home. I recognized Georgetown as we crossed M Street and began to drive through the narrow, old, tree-lined, cobblestone streets. There were the familiar wide boulevards and white stone high rises on both sides of the street. I noticed the crowds of yesterday were gone—except around the church. Across the street from the church, people were jammed together in long lines, four to five feet deep.

It was 8:30 am when we arrived. The ceremony was scheduled to commence at 9:30 am. Inside the church, Mr. Joshua Dubois, the 26-year-old director of Obama's Religious Outreach Strategy, met us. He had worked for Obama in his Senate office. (On February 5, 2009, he was appointed Director of the newly named Council for Faith Based and Neighborhood Partnerships.) I ran into Eric Holder as we were being led down the long aisle on the right side of the church. He wasn't very friendly. Perhaps he was preoccupied with his newly appointed cabinet post and the upcoming Congressional hearings. Or, maybe that was just his decorum, which can sometimes be quite different than what's inside of a person. However, in the present climate of friendliness, smiles, handshakes, hugs, and kisses, his cold, distant behavior stood out like the proverbial sore thumb. It should be said that at his swearing-in, when he was greeted with hoots and howls and a standing ovation, he showed no emotion. Nor did he show any emotion during the actual swearing-in, nor after his speech.

The section reserved for the clergy was adjacent to the stage where program participants were seated. Our seats were close to the proceedings and we had an excellent view of the dignitaries who sat on the front seats. The one problem with our seats was that we found ourselves always looking at the backs and the sides of the participants. So finally, we had our seats changed to the center of the church. Dr. Obery Hendricks, Professor at New York Theological Seminary, joined us.

The Congressional section was located across the nave. As we settled in our seats, Senator John McCain, followed by Senator Joe Lieberman, walked down the aisle. They looked so small, so ordinary. But this is usually true of the high and the mighty. The closer we get, the more human and ordinary they appear. This is probably the primary reason we, (and the people love to have it so) wrap ourselves in symbolisms of power and importance. They, and we, need to be reminded that we are special.

The Cathedral is an interesting place. In 1792, land for a "great church for national purposes" was set-aside in Pierre L'Enfant's Plan of the Federal City. The National Portrait Gallery now occupies that site. In 1891, a meeting was held to renew plans for a National Cathedral.

James Forman, who began his demand for reparations from religious houses of worship in 1969, used the Riverside Church in New York to launch his platform. He claimed that religious institutions had benefited from slavery by direct involvement and/or via governmental and/or private gifts that had been derived from the slave trade.

Construction of the cathedral started on September 29, 1907 with a ceremonial address by President Theodore Roosevelt and the laying of the cornerstone. In 1912, Bethlehem Chapel opened for services in the unfinished cathedral and these services have continued, daily, ever since.

When construction of the cathedral resumed after a brief hiatus for the First World War, architects Bodley and Vaughan had passed away. American architect Philip Hubert Frohman took over the design of the cathedral.

Washington National Cathedral was finally completed on September 29, 1990, after almost a century of planning and 83 years of construction. It was funded entirely from private sources; maintenance and upkeep continue to rely upon private support.

Washington National Cathedral was the site of two Presidential state funerals. The first was for Dwight D. Eisenhower. The second was for Ronald W. Reagan. There was also the Presidential burial of Woodrow Wilson, who was buried in the cathedral mausoleum.

Eisenhower lay in repose at the cathedral before lying in state. In addition, a memorial service for Harry Truman took place at National Cathedral. Many foreign dignitaries attended it.

I attended two other events. The first was the Prayer Breakfast at the Washington National Cathedral, which was a 20-minute drive away from home. I recognized Georgetown as we crossed M Street and began to drive through the narrow, old, tree-lined, cobblestone streets. There were the familiar wide boulevards and white stone high rises on both sides of the street. I noticed the crowds of yesterday were gone—except around the church. Across the street from the church, people were jammed together in long lines, four to five feet deep.

It was 8:30 am when we arrived. The ceremony was scheduled to commence at 9:30 am. Inside the church, Mr. Joshua Dubois, the 26-year-old director of Obama's Religious Outreach Strategy, met us. He had worked for Obama in his Senate office. (On February 5, 2009, he was appointed Director of the newly named Council for Faith Based and Neighborhood Partnerships.) I ran into Eric Holder as we were being led down the long aisle on the right side of the church. He wasn't very friendly. Perhaps he was preoccupied with his newly appointed cabinet post and the upcoming Congressional hearings. Or, maybe that was just his decorum, which can sometimes be quite different than what's inside of a person. However, in the present climate of friendliness, smiles, handshakes, hugs, and kisses, his cold, distant behavior stood out like the proverbial sore thumb. It should be said that at his swearing-in, when he was greeted with hoots and howls and a standing ovation, he showed no emotion. Nor did he show any emotion during the actual swearing-in, nor after his speech.

The section reserved for the clergy was adjacent to the stage where program participants were seated. Our seats were close to the proceedings and we had an excellent view of the dignitaries who sat on the front seats. The one problem with our seats was that we found ourselves always looking at the backs and the sides of the participants. So finally, we had our seats changed to the center of the church. Dr. Obery Hendricks, Professor at New York Theological Seminary, joined us.

The Congressional section was located across the nave. As we settled in our seats, Senator John McCain, followed by Senator Joe Lieberman, walked down the aisle. They looked so small, so ordinary. But this is usually true of the high and the mighty. The closer we get, the more human and ordinary they appear. This is probably the primary reason we, (and the people love to have it so) wrap ourselves in symbolisms of power and importance. They, and we, need to be reminded that we are special.

The Cathedral is an interesting place. In 1792, land for a "great church for national purposes" was set-aside in Pierre L'Enfant's Plan of the Federal City. The National Portrait Gallery now occupies that site. In 1891, a meeting was held to renew plans for a National Cathedral.

James Forman, who began his demand for reparations from religious houses of worship in 1969, used the Riverside Church in New York to launch his platform. He claimed that religious institutions had benefited from slavery by direct involvement and/or via governmental and/or private gifts that had been derived from the slave trade.

Construction of the cathedral started on September 29, 1907 with a ceremonial address by President Theodore Roosevelt and the laying of the cornerstone. In 1912, Bethlehem Chapel opened for services in the unfinished cathedral and these services have continued, daily, ever since.

When construction of the cathedral resumed after a brief hiatus for the First World War, architects Bodley and Vaughan had passed away. American architect Philip Hubert Frohman took over the design of the cathedral.

Washington National Cathedral was finally completed on September 29, 1990, after almost a century of planning and 83 years of construction. It was funded entirely from private sources; maintenance and upkeep continue to rely upon private support.

Washington National Cathedral was the site of two Presidential state funerals. The first was for Dwight D. Eisenhower. The second was for Ronald W. Reagan. There was also the Presidential burial of Woodrow Wilson, who was buried in the cathedral mausoleum.

Eisenhower lay in repose at the cathedral before lying in state. In addition, a memorial service for Harry Truman took place at National Cathedral. Many foreign dignitaries attended it.

• • •

Daily Challenge WEEKEND EDITION,
FEBRUARY 20-22, 2009

JANUARY 21
THE NATIONAL PRAYER SERVICE

THIS EPISCOPAL CHURCH IS SIMILAR TO THE GOTHIC STRUCTURES seen throughout Christendom in Europe. I began to reflect on the great cathedrals in which I had preached, prayed, and visited: Notre Dame in Paris; St. Peter's in Rome; Westminster Abbey in London; Canterbury in Canterbury, where King Henry II had his former friend, Bishop Thomas Becket, stabbed to death at the altar, St. John the Divine; and Riverside Church in New York City. The last time I spoke at the Riverside Church was in 2003. I had just returned from leading an interfaith, interracial delegation to Iraq, two weeks before the bombing started. It was a last desperate attempt to achieve peace. My trip reinforced my opposition to the war.

I've always felt overwhelmed, smothered, and swallowed up by these above-mentioned, beautifully designed, mammoth piles of stone. Perhaps, that is the point. Perhaps the cathedral represents the All Mighty Creator. Hence, they should make humans feel insignificant. Yes, the structures are awe-inspiring, but they are minus a feeling of warmth, life, flesh, and blood.

My feelings are nondiscriminatory. I feel the same way in all colossal religious houses where the Gods of these worship places are said to dwell. I find it hard to associate the God of these canyons of steel and stone with the poor, homeless, diseased, forlorn and forgotten persons who usually nearby encircle them. This is not to suggest that they don't do good works. In most instances their magnanimity is deep and comprehensive. It's just hard for me to reconcile the massive structure with the least in society.

The images of holy places I saw in three cities are representative of holy places I have seen and/or visited across the globe. In Calcutta, India, the low point of human suffering, I stood outside the gate of a massive, sprawling, gleaming white church, surrounded by high gleaming white walls, enclosing fresh, green, manicured lawns. The place was encircled and teeming with beggars. There were deformed, dirty, ragged humans of every age and every description. I thought about Mother Teresa who gave her life working among these poor, pathetic, diseased children of God. My admiration and appreciation for her was deepened.

In Nairobi, Kenya, I observed as the imams sat on the steps of a huge, colorful mosque and watched dirty, little, ragged children scurrying for bread. They never moved. They showed no compassion. It was as if this was the normal daily occurrence.

In Bangkok, Thailand, I visited pagodas where buddhas of all sizes sat or reclined, and were usually made or bedecked with expensive jewelry. And close by, impoverished, emaciated, diseased humans, lived in broken-down, dilapidated shacks surrounded by unspeakable filth, surviving on little to nothing.

Significantly, I'm told that the church administration of the National Cathedral writes the programs, according to its guidelines, for everything done in the church. As I studied the program, two things caught my attention. Firstly, there were many references to the New Testament along with many Christian words and symbols. When some Jewish leaders participate in an interfaith ceremony, they require the absence of the name of Jesus Christ and a minimization of Christian references. Secondly, there were a great number of participants, twenty to be exact. It must have required extraordinary imagination to involve so many distinguished men and women of God in one ceremony

There were four preludes: Carillon, Organ, Brass, and Chorale. The Washington Performing Arts Society Children of the Gospel Choir performed the Choral Prelude. They sang a medley of four tunes and rehearsed us singing, "He Got the Whole World in His Hands." When the ceremony started, we were told we would be asked to sing the above song with them.

Daily Challenge WEDNESDAY, FEBRUARY 25, 2009

JANUARY 21
THE PRAYER SERICE

CONCLUSION

AT 9:35 AM, FORMER PRESIDENT AND NEW SECRETARY OF STATE, William and Hillary Clinton entered the sanctuary. The huge cavernous church grew silent – the silence seemed to deepen with every passing second. It was obvious who was about to enter. Firstly, there was Mrs. Obama, with the two children. Then, a thunderous applause reverberated across the church as President Barack Obama entered. They entered near the section we had just left and sat on the front row across the aisle. Had we remained where we were, we would've had an ideal view facing the VIPs, including the first family.

The long procession of horns and flags and colorfully clad clergy slowly marched down the nave to their assigned seats while the congregation sang "Holy, Holy, Holy, Lord God Almighty…"

The Reverend Samuel T. Lloyd III delivered the welcome address. He captured my imagination when he said, "Dr. King spoke from this very place," pointing to where he was standing. "A week before he was assassinated, he went from here to Memphis."

The memories of the Montgomery Bus Boycott in 1955; the stabbing in Harlem in the late '50s by a crazed woman as he was book signing; the freedom rides in the early '60s; Operation C (Confrontation) the campaign in Birmingham: fire hoses, police dogs, and jailing children; the march on Washington and the "I Have a Dream" speech in 1963; the Nobel Peace Prize in 1964; the Alabama March and Bloody Sunday on the Edmund Pettus Bridge 1965 in Selma; the voter and civil rights legislations 1965; a continuation of the James Meredith march against fear in Mississippi and the Black power debate with Kwame Toure along the way; in the '60s there were the civil rights martyrs and victims of racist violence, Jimmy Lee Jackson and Rev. James Reeves and Medgar Evers, Andrew Goodman, James Chany, Micky Schwerner, Viola Luizzo; the three children killed the church bombing; and even before all the above 14-year-old, Emit Till 1954 to name but a few; Vietnam war speech at the Riverside Church in New York where I sat enthralled as he spoke out against the Vietnam War; organizing for the Poor People's campaign and Resurrection City in the late 1960s; garbage worker's strike and mass rallies; The Masonic Temple rally; the mountain top speech, guaranteeing the promised land; the Lorraine hotel, Dr. King standing on the balcony, then prostrate on the floor, bleeding with a white napkin or handkerchief on the side of his neck and face; followers weeping and pointing in the distance—and on and on, the phantasmagoria continued.

Dr. Otis Moss brought my thoughts back to the cathedral for awhile. I've always had great respect for him. He's an impressive man, in a quiet way. The welcome, the sermon and Dr. Moss' prayer were the only unscripted part of the ceremony. As was his custom, he slowly came to the microphone and began his invocation. In between the long pauses, my mind went on another trip.

Dr. Moss and I had both been seated at the breakfast table with President Clinton in the State Room at the White House for the last of the periodic prayer breakfast the President would have with about 120 interfaith religious leaders.

After more prayers, readings, and music, Dr. Wintley Phipps sang "Amazing Grace." His smooth melodious baritone voice sent my mind wandering back to the 1984 Democratic Convention in San Francisco. Rev. Jesse Jackson had made a great run for the Presidency. I still believe he never got the credit for his contributions, especially in the political area. We came up with the term "Rainbow Coalition" during the '84 campaign. It represented the wide diversity of the people participating in the campaign. It is unfair and inaccurate to say Jesse ran a campaign confined to race. He was always reaching out to all nationalities, religions, classes, etc. At the same time, it is true he never minimized his racial identity or where the base of his support came. After his convention speech, Jesse introduced Dr. Phipps who was great then. He was even greater this morning.

Reverend Dr. Sharon E. Watkins delivered the sermon. She made history by being the first woman to address the national prayer serevice. She challenged the President to sustain his values and principles and to always consider those at the bottom. If you provide for the needy, people will see God in the act. She told the story of an elderly Indian man encouraging a youth to pursue the right path in life. The youth asked the elder, "How will I know which way to travel?" The old man replied, "There are two wolves inside of you, a good wolf and a bad wolf, each one striving to get control. Whichever wolf you feed, will be the stronger and will force you to go his way." It was 11:23 am when the ceremony ended.

Outside, the crowds on the street were still large. They were waiting, milling around, hoping to catch a glimpse of the President, and trying to savor every moment. The tight security forced us to walk several blocks to our waiting car.

This would probably be our last ride with Mr. Singh. His car service had been retained by the DNC. He is a super-courteous and caring East Indian. We were now headed to the Marriott Hotel, about 20 minutes away, for the last official meeting of Chairman Dean's administration as head of the Democratic National Committee.

Daily Challenge WEEKEND EDITION,
FEBRUARY 27–MARCH 1, 2009

JANUARY 21: THE CHANGE OF LEADERSHIP AT THE DNC

THE LAST TIME I WAS AT THIS HOTEL, MAY 31, 2008, PICKET signs and demonstrators had surrounded the place. It was during the DNC Rules and Bylaws Committee meeting, where a compromise was forged regarding the seating of Michigan's and Florida's delegates to the Convention. (See Chapter One.)

Fast forward eight months, and inside the hotel, the DNC had set up a string of offices on the 1st floor. We went directly to a private room where the always-friendly Chairman Howard Dean and staff were waiting. We greeted each other with broad smiles, a handshake, and an embrace. Virginia Governor Tim Kaine joined later and the two men reviewed the final details for the farewell ceremony to follow.

The huge ballroom was two-thirds filled with DNC members, political bigwigs, staff, and supporters. After the usual preliminaries, Gov. Dean made his goodbye speech. Always pleasant and energetic, he thanked the staff and delegates for their support. He profusely praised his successor, Gov. Kaine, and was given a prolonged standing ovation.

He descended the stage, still smiling and waving and took his seat between Mrs. Kaine and me. Leah had arranged this seat of honor for Rennie and me.

I instinctively liked Governor Dean from the first time I met him. I was impressed with his friendliness, brilliance, creativity, energy, compassion, and his praise and elevating of others. He really enhanced my admiration in May 2006 during the DNC meeting in New Orleans, held after Hurricane Katrina. The DNC decided that they should spend a day helping in the rebuilding efforts. Governor Dean and I worked on a house that had been devastated by the flood. Thinking it would be just a photo-op, I was shocked to see him actually working. He disregarded pleas to put on a mask and other protective clothing, or to stop or at least slow down in his labor. He worked nonstop for hours. In fact, even after I had stopped, he continued.

He treated Leah with respect and admiration, giving her his full trust and confidence. He allowed her the freedom to be innovative. They made a great team and had phenomenal success. Under Dean's leadership, a number of governorships, and both houses of Congress were won. And most of all, the White House was won. It was with Dean's 50-state strategy, along with Leah's religious outreach (which they implemented against stiff resistance) that Obama continued to his astounding victory.

When Governor Dean settled down, I thanked him for the support and friendship he gave Leah. Always self-effacing, praising others, he said, "Thanks belongs to Leah. She is the one who deserves the praise. She did the work."

When the new Chair gave his acceptance speech, he returned Governor Dean's compliment. He recounted all of Dean's successes. I kept saying to myself, I hope he tells this to his boss and his boss' boss or advisers. And I hope he asks why Dean had not been given greater consideration in the

Obama administration. Gov Kaine laid out his three-point program:

- To support the President's agenda.
- To carry the banner of fighting for people's rights.
- To engage with the American people in new ways

I liked him. I felt he was a decent human being. Leah confirmed my feelings. She said, "He is a good man." His credentials were impressive, especially his work as a missionary in Honduras, and as a civil rights attorney. It is important to note that when Kaine was running for Governor back in 2005, he was the first beneficiary of Governor Dean's 50-state strategy, with the DNC giving $5 million to help him win the election. It was a major win and it confirmed Governor Dean's belief that the Democrats could win in any state.

Daily Challenge WEDNESDAY EDITION, MARCH 4, 2009

JANUARY 21: THE CHANGE OF LEADERSHIP AT THE DNC

CONCLUSION

DONNA BRAZILE WAS ELECTED VICE CHAIR OF THE DNC; DR. Obery Hendricks gave the benediction and, just like that, another great moment in history passed into memory. As I sat next to Governor Dean, it was hard to digest reality. A few hours earlier, I'd been at the National Prayer Service with some of the most powerful people on earth, including the President in his first full day in office. And Governor Dean, a little while before, had been head of the DNC, the architect of his party's dramatic recapture of power. Now his term was concluded and he was jobless. The person who was now speaking, whose smiling wife sat one person away from me, was the Chairperson of the party and Ms. Donna Brazile was the Vice Chair. (When I first met Donna, she was a 20-year-old activist and I was the Chair of the National Black United Front. We worked together again when she was a youth worker in Jackson Presidential campaign of '84.)

Across the aisle, in the front row, sat Rev. Willie Barrow, a DNC member with a long history in the Civil Rights Movement. It was she who introduced Rev. Jackson to Dr. MLK Jr. And with my grandson, Rennie, seated next to me, representative of the future, and my daughter Leah close by, moving around, observing, analyzing and orchestrating everything, it all seem unreal. It was as though my life had gone full cycle in a matter of hours.

Delightfully, I finished my Washington journey with Leah and Rennie, eating dinner in Union Station. The crowd everywhere seemed to have returned to normalcy—except at B. Smith's restaurant in the station. I was looking forward to feasting on barbecue ribs (soy). Before I became vegan, I had a national reputation as a connoisseur of barbecue ribs. B's had the closest taste to the real thing. But the restaurant was booked, a consequence of the lingering crowd. I selfishly wished they would all go home so I could have my barbecue. Instead, we settled for America, a nearby restaurant in Union Station. But when you're with people you love, enmeshed in conversation regarding important events and people, eating becomes secondary, at least that's the way I feel. The people and the moment are what's important.

While dining, as God would have it, it was discovered that we were seated next to a friend of Leah's, who is a chief staff person for one of the recently appointed cabinet members.

When we were introduced, he said to me, "Leah has talked about you often, especially during the convention in Denver." I can't think of a more satisfying conclusion to a week of unforgettable experiences, than to hear that your children think highly of you and speak of you in the wide circles in which they interact.

The 7:55 pm train was on time. Unlike my trip to D.C., I had two seats to myself. It was after 1:00 am when I arrived home. Thus, Washington and the week of important people and events ended just as it began—in bed. All things human, at some point, return to sleep. Ultimately, what we did when we were awake determines whether that is good or bad. According to some religious teachings, when we are awakened on this side of history or the other side, we will carry with us and be shaped by the experiences of the day and years before.

So, I fell asleep as I often do, reciting the prayer of my childhood. *"Now I lay me down to sleep. I pray the Lord my soul to keep. If I should die before I wake, I pray the Lord my soul to take."* And I will face the morning as I usually do, with the words from the Sanskrit,

> *Look well to this day, for it is life, the very life of life.*
> *In it lays all the realities and verities of existence:*
> *the bliss of growth, the glory of action, and splendor*
> *of beauty. For yesterday is but a dream, and tomorrow*
> *only a vision. But today well-lived makes every*
> *yesterday a dream of happiness and every tomorrow*
> *a vision of hope. Look well, therefore, to this day,*
> *for it and it alone is life! Such is the salutation of*
> *the dawn.*

APPENDICES

Daily Challenge WEDNESDAY, JANUARY 21, 2009

EXCERPT FROM A SPEECH I DID FOR THE ENVIRONMENTAL PROTECTION AGENCY ON JANUARY 14, 2009

PART ONE

THE SUBJECT YOU HAVE CHOSEN, LIVING THE DREAM, PRESENTS a towering challenge if by living the dream you mean putting into practice, in our everyday living, the ideals that Dr. Martin Luther King Jr. impassionedly articulated in what is called the "I Have a Dream" speech. Lest we be mesmerized by the poetic beauty of Dr. King's words and hasten to embrace the high sounding ideals, only to discover later, to our dismay and/or guilt we're not up to the task, let us go back and hear again his words, ponder his dreams, and then ask ourselves if we understand?

Am I ready? Am I willing? Am I able? Am I ready to say "Yes" to the dream? Am I willing to go forward this day, putting into practice the meaning of the dream? And, am I able to resist the detractors, deniers, and destroyers of the dream? Am I able to stand against the fiery darts of the critics of the dream? Am I able to say "No" to the seduction that will promise an easier path and/or financial and/or promotional rewards for turning away from the dream? In a word, are you able to make the sacrifice, bear the burden, go the distance, stand alone or join with the like minded, though they may be the majority or the few? If so, if you are able, the dream of Dr. King will be completely actualized in our time. What was the dream?

How distinctly I remember. It was 45 years ago, August 28, 1963. The mobilization for the rally had been building for a long time and all roads led to Washington, D.C. I was caught in a dilemma. On August 27th, Leah Denyatta, our first-born, arrived. Should I go to Washington, D.C. or stay home with my family? I decided for the family. I am not sure if that was the right decision. Dick Gregory said it was. He told me that he had a son who was born at the same time and he decided that he would go to Washington. Then, he said, "I've not seen my son since."

The parade of speakers, including Roy Wilkins, Executive Director of the National Association for the Advancement of Colored People (NAACP); Whitney Young, Executive Director Of Urban League (UL); James Forman, Executive Director of the Congress of Racial Equality (CORE); A. Philip Randolph, Head of the Brotherhood of Sleeping Car Porters (HBSCP), and John Lewis, Executive Director of the Student Nonviolent Coordinating Committee (SNCC) spoke eloquently, calling for civil rights, justice, equality, etc. Anticipation steadily swelled as the program moved towards its conclusion.

It was a sultry summer day. The crowd was getting restless. Patience was wearing thin. An estimated 250,000 had gathered at the Lincoln Memorial. They had come from all parts of the country and even from abroad. They had heard speeches and music. And now they were anxiously awaiting the man of the hour. Then he was introduced. The man and the moment had met. His words would help to move the nation from a "jangling discord to a beautiful symphony." Those who saw and heard him knew that they were in the presence of the kyrios (a Greek word meaning a divine moment, a God intervention, a special time). We knew we would never forget, nor would the nation forget.

Slowly, as was his style of speaking, he began:

> *I am happy to join with you today in what will go down in history as the greatest demonstration for freedom in the history of our nation.*
>
> *Five score years ago, a great American, in whose symbolic shadow we stand today, signed the Emancipation Proclamation. This momentous decree came as a great beacon light of hope to millions of Negro slaves who had been seared in the flames of withering injustice. It came as a joyous daybreak to end the long night of their captivity.*
>
> *But one hundred years later, the Negro still is not free. ... One hundred years later, the Negro lives on a lonely island of poverty in the midst of a vast ocean of material prosperity. One hundred years later, the Negro is still languished in the corners of American society and finds himself an exile in his own land. And so we've come here today to dramatize a shameful condition.*

And then he moved rhythmically, carrying the crowd with him, toward the articulation of his dream. And here is where he, and I, and you, face a challenge to actualize his dream.

Standing between two NAACP security guards, (One happens to be Charlie Jackson, my brother Bob's brother-in-law) his voice, rising and falling in a perfect cadence, his chest seeming to swell, and his body language inextricably woven into his words, his eyes peering, as though seeing beyond the present, he said,

> *I say to you today, my friends, that even though we face the difficulties today and tomorrow, I still have a dream. It is dream rooted in the American dream.... I have a dream that one day this nation will rise up and live out the true meaning of its*

> creed: "We hold these truths to be self-evident, that all men are created equal."

(King left out, "and endowed by the Creator with certain inalienable rights, that among these life, liberty, and the pursuit of happiness.")

Are we ready, willing, and able to live the dream of working and struggling for equality?

> I have a dream that one day on the red hills of Georgia, the sons of former slaves and the sons of former slave owners will be able to sit down together at the table of brotherhood.

Are we ready, willing, and able to live the dream as brothers and sisters?

> I have a dream that one day even the state of Mississippi, a state sweltering with the heat of injustice, sweltering with the heat of oppression, will be transformed into an oasis of freedom and justice.

Are we ready, willing, and able to live the dream to do all we can for freedom and justice even in the most hostile environments?

I have a dream that my four little children will one day live in a nation where they will not be judged by the color of their skin but by the content of their character.

Are we ready, willing, and able to live the dream of a society of mutual respect for human worth and values?

I have a dream that one day, down in Alabama, with its vicious racists, with its Governor having his lips dripping with the words of "interposition" and "nullification" -- one day right there in Alabama, little black boys and black girls will be able to join hands with little white boys and white girls as sisters and brothers.

Are you ready, willing, and able to live the dream of bringing into reality the beloved community?

I have a dream that one day every valley shall be exalted, and every hill and mountain shall be made low, the rough places will be made plain, and the crooked places will be made straight; "and the glory of the Lord shall be revealed and all flesh shall see it together.

Are you ready, willing, and able to live the dream of a fully democratic society?

Daily Challenge WEEKEND EDITION,
JANUARY 23 – 25, 2009

PART TWO

I KNOW THAT DR. KING HAS BEEN CALLED THE APOSTLE OF peace and the leader of non-violence. And although these designations are accurate, they sometimes, too often I think, rob Dr. King of his militancy and radicalism. We have, too many of us across the years, become narcotized or fixated on the dream and we have missed the challenges of the dream. Let us consider again the last dream. "I have a dream that one day every valley shall be exalted, and every hill and mountain shall be made low, the rough places will be made plain, and the crooked places will be made straight; "and the glory of the Lord shall be revealed and all flesh shall see it together." This dream comes from a Biblical passage located in Isaiah 40:4. It is clear from the biblical reference that the Prophet and therefore Dr. King was not speaking of the physical aspects of the earth. Rather, he was poetically expressing an ideal state of human society. The dream or the hope expressed is that one day there will be a complete democratization of society. Those in high places will be brought down. Those in low places will be lifted up and things that are crooked will be made straight. The rough places will be made smoothed and the glory of the Lord will be seen in the Valley. And all flesh shall see it together. When the time comes that freedom, equality of opportunities, a complete political, economic, and social equalization prevails in the world, indeed we will all see God.

It calls to mind the promise that in the last day, God would pour out of his spirit upon all flesh. That day was fulfilled on the day of Pentecost, when according to the Bible, the people were filled with the Holy Ghost. By the way, this is where those who name themselves Pentecostal, respective to their religious denomination, derive their meaning and origin. Pentecost was an experience, not a denomination. In the 19th century, those who had the Pentecostal experience were forced to form denominations.

Make no mistake about it, Dr. King was a radical in the true meaning of the term. The definition of the Latin root of the word radical is getting to the core of things. He once called for a radical redistribution of political and economic power. The poor people's campaign in Washington, which some people think got him killed in 1967, was a revolutionary act. His intention was to stay in Washington with representatives of the impoverished and their supporters, until the Nation delivered on its promise.

History demands that we remember there was another voice in Washington in 1963. Malcolm X said that while Dr. King was dreaming, masses of black people were having nightmares. In actuality, both of them were right. Disturbing images do come into dreams. In 1963, racism was very much alive. Unemployment was pervasive and economic disparities were glaring. And so it is today. We are in a time of severe economic crisis. Unemployment has hit double figures. The financial institutions we thought were forever have collapsed. Homes that have been in the family for years, homes we thought we would pass on to future generations, are being taken from us and war seem to be everywhere. Yes, these are crisis times. However, if Dr. King were here, I believe he would say, "But I still have a dream."

Today, there is a lot to encourage us to live the dream. We have seen great strides towards the realization of the dream. Inarguably, we still have a long way to go. But, we cannot deny, indeed we must not deny, that significant gains have been made. To deny the gains would be to say that the sacrifice and struggle of those who have gone before, and even those who have struggled in our own time, have been in vain.

Who would have thought that we in New York would have lived to see an African American Governor, David Paterson? (Even his coming to the Governorship was through peculiar circumstances.) Who would have thought that we would live to see a Majority Leader of the State Senate, Malcolm Smith, and Chair of the Ways and Means Committee, Charlie Rangel all serving at the same time? And then there's the black, Brooklyn-born, C.E.O. of the 2008 Democratic Convention in Denver, daughter of our church and community. This same lady who was born 45 years ago has been the Chief of Staff of the DNC for the last six and a half years and was appointed to organize the Convention. And wonder of wonders, who would've ever thought we would live to see a black President with a strange sounding-name, mixed parentage, and relatively new to the scene? Significant numbers elected this man, Barack Hussein Obama, overwhelmingly from a broad cross section of the American population. This is dreamy stuff.

These are exciting times in which we live. The possibilities are endless. All of us should accept the challenge of Ralph Waldo Emerson, to "hitch our wagons to a star." We have the opportunities that our mothers, fathers, and freedom fighters gave their lives to make possible.

Open letter to the Black Press

"Let Our Pens and Our Voices Tell the Stories of Our Achievers"

by
Reverend Herbert Daughtry

Pardon me, but I cannot contain my anger, disappointment and frustration any longer. On August 28th, 2008, The Democratic National Convention in Denver, Colorado came to an end. The assessments from veteran participants and observers consistently ranged from comments such as "this was one of the best" to "it was the best." Even the media, black and white, joined the chorus of praises.

I'm proud to say that Reverend Leah Daughtry, who, as I think most of you know, is my eldest daughter, led the Convention as its Chief Executive Officer. (But even if she were not my daughter, I would be writing the same letter.)

Leah was born in Brooklyn and grew up in our House of the Lord Church and community. She held several senior posts in the

Clinton Administration, including Senior Advisor to the Secretary of Labor, Chief of Staff, and finally Assistant Secretary (acting) of Labor for Administration and Management, with responsibility for the department's $35 million budget. Since 2002, she has served as Chief of Staff for the Democratic National Committee. During the 1992 election cycle, she held the position of Managing Director of the Democratic National Convention. She is the fifth generation of ministers in our family, and is the founding pastor of The House of the Lord Church in Washington, D.C.

Yet, in spite of Leah's history and accomplishments, there has been little written in the black press about her accomplishments prior to the convention and nothing since. While the white press, such as Newsweek and the New York Times Sunday Magazine, devoted significant ink to Leah, I saw nothing comparable in our black national magazines like Ebony and Essence.

Although Essence Magazine ran a small piece about Leah, it was in connection with the not-for-profit youth work she'd previously done for our Church's community service agency. But incredibly, there has been nothing in the New York black press, except in the Daily Challenge, which primarily carried photos. And there was an article in the Amsterdam News many months prior to the convention.

Now here is what angers, disappoints, and frustrates me the most: If Leah had been caught selling or using dope, or in a prostitution ring, or stealing money, or engaged in some form of violence either as the victim or the perpetrator; if the convention had failed dismally and/or Leah had been accused of incompetence; if she had been accused of malfeasance or misappropriation of money, it would had been headlined across the front pages with detailed, lurid stories. In fact, there would probably have been a series of articles and a periodic update of the story.

So why in the name of God, decency, fairness and inspiration haven't you, the black press, devoted at least as much coverage to our achievers as you do to our underachievers, non-achievers, or the negatives in our community, especially for the sake of our youth? Why haven't you written a little something about this young woman (and so many other of our achievers) who calls herself a "black chick from Brooklyn" and has accomplished so much, not the least of which is being the Chief Executive Officer of the greatest Democratic Convention ever?

If there were stories I missed, pardon my oversight. Now having said that, I still believe that Leah's achievement was so phenomenal that the story should have been written in such a way that nobody could've missed it.

INDEX

Akintayo, Tina, 48
Alexander, Elizabeth, 150
Ali, Muhammad, 71

Bailey, A. Peter, XVI
Barron, Charles, 31, 118
Barrow, Willie, 143, 166
Berry, Halle, 143
Joe Biden, 42, 69, 71, 73, 80, 84
Blake, Charles Sr., 50
Booker, Corey, 38, 68
Donna Brazile, 25, 57, 166
Brown, Lila, 117
Brown, Ron, 10
Bush, George H. W., 96
Bush, George W., 81

Carter, Jimmy, 72
Chavis, Ben, 13
Chambers, Lorenzo Daughtry, V, XI, 48, 131, 147
Clark, Yvette, 57
Clinton, Bill, 11, 18, 69, 71, 72, 73
Clinton, Hillary, 7, 9, 10, 29, 31, 63, 65, 66, 68, 69, 73, 80, 97, 138, 160
Colorado Convention Center, 63, 70, 75
Convention
  African American Caucus, 54, 70
  Credentials, 45, 46, 47, 48, 55, 63, 64, 75, 76, 165
  Denver, 10, 21, 24, 35, 36, 37,

38, 39, 40, 51, 52, 74,
79, 86, 106, 148, 167,
175, 176
Faith Caucus, 54, 64
Pepsi Center, 38, 46, 47, 58,
73, 75
Roll Call Vote, 69
Skyboxes, 40, 45, 47

Darfur, 45, 133
Daughtry, Herbert Jr., V, 60
Daughtry, Karen Smith, 118
Daughtry, Leah D., V, XI,
XVI, XVIII, 10, 12, 33,
34, 36, 37, 38, 39, 40,
41, 45, 46, 47, 48, 49,
50, 51, 53, 54, 55, 56,
57, 59, 60, 61, 63, 64,
70, 71, 73, 74, 75, 76,
77, 82, 83, 85, 86, 106,
122, 141, 148, 151, 164,
165, 166, 167, 170, 176,
177, 178
Daughtry, Sharon, V, XI, 33,
38, 46, 48, 60, 64, 76,
162
Dawn, IV, X, 33, 38, 48,
60, 79
Davis, Lanny, 25
Dean, Howard, 10, 37, 38, 39,
59, 85, 163
Democratic National Committee
(DNC), 10, 38, 130
Florida, 18, 19, 21, 24,
65, 95, 97, 122, 123,
141, 163
Michigan, 18, 19, 21, 24,
65, 163
Rules and Bylaws Committee
18, 19, 21, 24, 163
Democratic Party, XV, 8, 12,
15, 20, 21, 22, 24, 29,
34, 39, 53, 59, 67, 79,
104, 110
Democratic Primaries
Florida, 18, 19, 21, 24, 65,
95, 97, 122, 123, 141,
163
Michigan, 18, 19, 21, 24,
65, 163
Potomac Primary, 13
Super Tuesday, XVI, 3, 13,
15, 30
Denver Colorado
Hotel Teatro, 37, 38
Invesco Field, 74, 79
Pepsi Center, 38, 46, 47, 58,
73, 75
DuBois, Joshua, 153, 155
DuBois, Maurice, 117

El Bashir, Omar, 117, 133
Election Day, 109, 114, 116,
118, 122
Evans, Randolph, 57
Eve, Arthur, 132
Eve, Eric, 132

Faith in Action, 51, 53, 76
Faw, Bob, 121
Feinstein, Dianne, 29, 147
Florida, 18, 19, 21, 24, 65, 95,
97, 122, 123, 141, 163
Fowler, Don, 85

Franklin, Aretha, 147
Giuliani, Rudolph, 100
Gore, Al, 95

Herman, Alexis, 10, 21, 24, 35
Hickenlooper, John, 39
Hicks, H. Beecher Jr., 76
Hill, Winston, 71, 85, 88
Holder, Eric, 146, 153, 156
Holeman, Christine, 117
Hubbard, Wilma, 64
Hudson, Jennifer, 77

Ickes, Harold, 24
Interfaith Gathering, 49, 50
Invesco Field, 74, 79

Jackson, Jacqueline, 67
Jackson, Jesse Jr., 62, 67
Jackson, Reverend Jesse, 62, 67
Jesus Christ, XII, XV, 159
Jim Crow, 4
Johnson, Bob, 25

Kaine, Tim, 163
Kennedy, Ted, 30, 62, 80
Kerry, John, 30
Kilmer, Joyce, 32
King, Jerry XII, 117
King, Martin Luther Jr., 5, 71, 84, 110, 131, 132, 169
Ku Klux Klan, 101

Lee, Spike, 115
Lowery, Joseph, 57

Malcolm X, XVI, 110, 174

Mandela, Nelson, 10, 115
Martin, Roland, 59, 120
Mattson, Ingrid, 52
McAuliffe, Terry, 10, 30
McCain, John, 16, 81, 97, 99, 100, 105, 154, 156
McKinney, Cynthia, 89
Merida, Kevin, 78
Michigan, 18, 19, 21, 24, 65, 163
Mile High Stadium, 74
Moss, Otis, 161
Mother Teresa, 159

Nader, Ralph, 97
Norton, Eleanor Holmes, 66

Obama, Barack, 3, 9, 22, 30, 55, 63, 66, 68, 69, 72, 79, 84, 105, 116, 121, 123, 133, 136, 160
Obama, Michelle, 59, 63, 124
Ocompo, Luis Moreno, 133

Palin, Sarah, 87, 96
Paterson, David, 62, 175
Pelosi, Nancy, 73
Pepsi Center, 38, 46, 47, 58, 73, 75
Pfleger, Michael, 27
Phipps, Wintley, 162
Prejean, Helen, 50, 51, 52
Proctor, Dennis, 59

Rangel, Charlie, 25, 70, 175
Rendell, Ed, 25
Republican Party, 119

Richard Smallwood &
    Vision, 51
Ritter, Bill, 51
Roberts, John, 17
Roberts, John G., Jr., 147
Robinson, Annette M., 51
Romney, Mitt, 88
Roosevelt, James Jr., 21, 24
Rubie, Yvonne, 64

Salley, Columbus, 125
Sanford, Adelaide, 59, 76
Sharpton, Al, 145
Tom Skinner, 87
Smith, Linwood, 136
Smith, Malcolm, 73, 175
Sorensen, Ted, 66
Starks, Chyann, XII
Super Tuesday, XVI, 3, 13, 15,
    30, 180, 188
Swearing-in, 136, 149, 152-
    153, 156

Tutu, Desmond, 8
Total Worship Experience, 42,
    63
Towns, Ed, 10, 62, 70
Thompson, Willie, 62

Umpthery, Evangeline, 138

Vincent, Ayana, XI, 117

Wright, Bruce, 62, 69, 70, 95
West, Cornel, 6
Washington, Denzel, 115, 143
Watkins, Sharon E., 162

Weinreb, Tzvi Hersh, 51, 53
Wright, Jeremiah, 120, 124,
    138
Walker, Laverne, 64
Waters, Maxine, 89
Wilson, Gwendolyn, 117
Winfrey, Oprah, 122
Warren, Rick, 147
Watkins, Thomas Jr., XIII